The Medical Fitness
How to Reverse Chronic Disease While
Building Your Bottom Line

J.R. Burgess, MS Medical Impact Innovator

Forward: Dr. Joel Baumgartner, MD Medical Visionary

The current state and uncertainty the Healthcare System brings, has required diligent focus from physicians, private practices and hospital systems to formulate solutions. The current structure brings intense challenges for private practices to survive. With rising healthcare costs, reimbursements continue to experience cuts, leaving many medical systems vulnerable. The upside is that there is a large opportunity for practices to protect their futures by adding cash-based models and preventable care to their current standard. This model will restore health in patients and it is proving to mature at an extraordinary pace. In 2018, CMS will release "The Diabetes Prevention Program" (DPP) creating the first opportunity for preventative services such as personal training, health coaching, and wellness services to be covered by insurance.

Healthcare: Where Are We Now

- Obesity on the Rise
- Disease on the Rise
- Rx's Increase Yearly
- Healthcare Costs on the Rise
- Insurance Rates on Rise
- Deductibles on the Rise
- Reimbursements Decreasing
- Bundled Payments and Outcome Based Quality Measures
- Managed Care

Obesity Crisis

On the Rise in AMERICA - est. 1 in 2 by 2020.

Leading Cause of **PREVENTABLE** Death in the World and Now According to AMA is Considered a Disease.

Overweight Patients the Healthcare System 40% More than Healthy Patients.

As Reported in a Study from 2008, Physical Inactivity Cost the US Healthcare System More than $102 Billion Annually.

Spending in the U.S. for Prescription Drugs was $259.1 Billion in 2010, and is Projected to DOUBLE over the Next Decade.

(Kaiser Family Foundation)

The obesity epidemic and the incidence of disease and injury have forced the need for a preventable, medically integrated, outcome-based model of medical fitness. Today's crisis leads to an urgent new paradigm in healthcare delivery that will combat the rise in chronic disease and associated healthcare costs. It is our focus, along with numerous other affiliations such as the Medical Fitness Association and Medical Fitness Network, to facilitate bridging the gap between evidence-based health centered treatment and long-term disease prevention strategies.

We Incorporated Medical Fitness to Create Change in A Broken System:

The 6 step "Medical Fitness I.M.P.A.C.T. Plan" outlined in this message and developed at Rejuv Medical is the future of medicine. A little over eight years ago I opened Rejuv Medical. I was practicing at a large hospital based clinic. Days consisted of working long hours, with an overbooked schedule and little time or energy to spend with family. I felt that the quality of outcomes with many traditional services and medications were far from optimal. I was prescribing medications to get patients through the pain and didn't have an opportunity to fully treat them and guide them in a comprehensive manner to create health and change in their lives. I first opened Rejuv to operate as a small functional, regenerative medicine and aesthetics clinic. I made this decision because the hospital system I was employed by decided to close its doors. Fortunately, I had a following of previous patients and decided it was time to go all-in with an insurance based non-surgical orthopedics and sports medicine practice. It was time to treat patients "the right way." The goal was and continues to be to give patients the gift of true health, based on research and sound science.

The broad medical fitness vision I had begun to take shape when J.R. Burgess walked through my newly formed practice. While going though graduate school J.R. was a personal trainer at Gold's Gym and was seeking my help form a rugby injury that had plagued him for years. In our conversations, I found he was unhappy with the long-term financial outlook of personal training in a large corporate gym. He had just finished graduate school and was talking about a desire for a new career and was leaving the gym to go back to building water towers. J.R. held this position while he succeeded in his life to pay his way through school. He spoke of his passion to help individuals lose weight, who would otherwise struggle on their own. He loved the show "The Biggest Loser" and how the show utilized a medical approach to help those who were the most desperate.

During our conversations, I mentioned that I always had a vision to combine the science of medicine and the physiology and endocrinology of the body to develop a healthcare model that creates permanent changes and regeneration my patient's lives.

A model that could turn back the clock, heal degenerative disease and injury while restoring health and vitality to my patients.

During his second Prolotherapy appointment, I let him know that our conversations had me thinking about the impact of obesity on today's society. I have always taught and preached that we need to stop covering up the symptoms and the causes associated with each diagnosis. Cortisone does not repair the painful, arthritic knee, nor does diabetes medication make disease disappear. Prescribing one medication after another does not fix anything. It was time to abandon the Band-Aids and restore health. There was a great need to rectify the lifestyle behaviors that led patients to their current health status. The patient with bad knees was helpless until he lost the 50 pounds that was causing the arthritic joints. The diabetic patient was still going to have complications and be dependent on medication if he or she didn't lose weight and make positive lifestyle changes to change the endocrinology that was slowly killing them. All medical professionals know how much of an impact a healthy diet, proper exercise and healthy behavioral changes can have on someone's life.

It was the show "The Biggest Loser" that spearheaded J.R.'s and my conversations regarding how we could make a difference in the world. The show proved how powerful a doctor's message can be when telling patients that it's imperative that you focus on healthy lifestyle changes. Doctors are regarded as the highest authoritative source in today's society. The unfortunate part is when doctors tell patients to eat healthy and exercise, but they don't show patients the means or have systems to help patients make permanent lifestyle changes, nor do they have the time. Therefore, I look at my Medical Fitness Specialists (formerly known as personal trainers) as the key to making long lasting lifestyle and health changes. The MFS Team has several contact hours with each patient to help apply the healthy programs we created. Our goal through the education systems we've created is that each client graduates from them with the knowledge they are empowered to make long lasting change. One of our goals is to empower each one of our clients and patients to have practical knowledge on nutrition, exercise, anatomy, physiology, endocrinology, and psychology so they can in turn change the lives of their families, friends and communities.

My purpose is not to verbally attack the government, pharmaceutical companies or insurance companies who continue to advocate for dangerous procedures like gastric bypass, or doctors who write one prescription after another without fully counseling their patients on proper nutrition and exercise. My dedication is to make an impact large enough to get the attention needed to change the way the health system operates. To reverse and decrease chronic diseases that are killing our patients, families, and communities.

We need to change the healthcare delivery system to focus on prevention and reversal of disease and degeneration. The focus should be to empower our patients to take their health into their own hands through education, exercise, nutrition and healthy lifestyle management. Everything in our program is evidence-based. With the right professionals and the precise training, you can handle any patient with high-risk needs and give them the gift of long lasting health and vitality.

We have an obligation to help change the lives of millions. This model is the solution to helping individuals lose weight, optimize health and reverse degenerative disease without masking the root cause. It also will create an atmosphere of health that starts in your practice and spreads throughout your community.

In eight years, we have grown leaps and bounds, and are building momentum for a viable and long-lasting entity that will help society rebound from the current healthcare crisis. I found that we can market medical fitness completely different than traditional medical practices can. The world is hungry for healthy weight loss and people are fed up with quick fix gimmicks. Medically supervised weight loss and fitness programs created by a physician have a unique selling position that puts us in a category of one. It lends credibility that attracts those who have struggled to gain control over their weight for years.

It will forever be our mission to get the "Medical Fitness Impact Plan" covered by all insurance plans. It is the only way our health system can survive the "growing" disease epidemic.

Chapter 1

The Visionary and Innovator Implement a Mission for Change "Successful Physicians look for opportunities" ~

Shelly Reese, Medscape (from the article *Why Some Practices Are Wildly Successful*) October 22, 2012

When I first joined Rejuv, the team consisted of five employees. Now, seven years later, Rejuv Medical has four locations and employs 90 team members. Each team member is empowered to change the way healthcare is known and delivered. In addition, we have enriched 33 practices in four different countries, we have opened or added a 6 step, turn-key system we created and since named called "The Medical Fitness I.M.P.A.C.T. Plan" to change their communities for the better. Joining Dr. Baumgartner in January of 2010, my journey started as the "Implementer". This role also known as the Medical Fitness Coordinator responsible for assisting Dr. Baumgartner to propel his vision forward. My graduate studies held an intense focus on nutrition and sports management. Over the years I gained the reputation of being the "go-to" trainer at the Gold's Gym in the area for weight loss and nutrition accountability. I could guide, motivate and successfully bring multiple clients to a loss that brought them to healthier weight and lifestyle. I've always had the yearning to coach, naturally born with it.

I was confident I would benefit Dr. Baumgartner's patients to recognize success and facilitate the growth and development of future team members. We discussed rolling forward with the approach in the correct fashion, with proper diet and exercise to truly improve the lives of those we served. We developed a model that, through education, taught people to make the lasting lifestyle changes needed to optimize health and even reverse disease and degeneration.

The location for the Medical Fitness Coordinator (Trainer) role where I first started out was a small 10' x 8' space I called the "closet". A handful of my former clients came with me, so it truly was almost no cost to Dr. Baumgartner's practice other than my salary. In the mornings and evenings outside clinical hours I would utilize the hallways and lobby for walking lunges, movement based exercises and plyometrics. In just two months I had to bring on two new trainers, Christine B. and Rich S. The intensity of the programming and word of mouth developed so rapidly, a good problem arose. There was no room inside the clinic. We contracted with Snap Fitness, paying the monthly membership for each of our patients. When spring came, Rich and I would use the local High School football field and track for outdoor boot camps and sports performance training. The Physical Therapist traded rooms so I could train multiple people at one time and graduated to the 10'x14' room right next door.

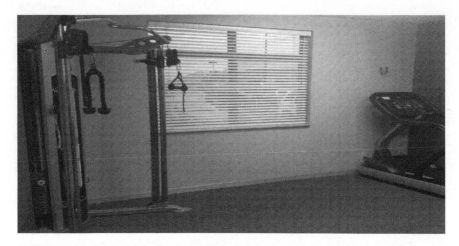

Eight months and 100 patients later we decided we needed to have our own standalone fitness center. Locating indoor space to keep our momentum going before the Minnesota winter hit full force became a highlight and necessary mission. At that time, the cost per membership we were paying at Snap would cover the overhead at a separate location. It would have been ideal to have the clinic and gym under the same roof, but given our leasing situation, that was not a possibility at the time. We sought out the most economical location I could find. A relator found us a 6,400-square-foot facility that we renovated in two months' time. This location allowed us to expand beyond personal training to include boot camps and group fitness. With the larger space, we grew rapidly in a very short time.

It has been just over seven years since I recall my first day of work. We now have improved the lives of over 2,500 patients make life giving changes. In the first 10 months before our standalone location, we were profitable because there was very little overhead. The first year at the Weight Loss & Performance Center we had nearly $180,000 in losses, as a standalone, due to the build out, new equipment, additional administrative support and day to day overhead expenses. Even though we lost due to the build out and equipment acquisition cost, the motivator is that the investment paid for itself. The new patients that came for the weight loss and fitness program generated over $300,000 in new revenue from the referrals to the clinic. It took exactly one year and one month to have our first profitable month as a standalone fitness facility. Still to this day we have utilized our fitness facility as the entry point and marketing focus to bring in new patients into our clinic that are ready for a positive long-term lifestyle change.

In a very short time-frame both our fitness center and clinic grew at a rapid pace. The original goal was not to create a master plan of driving fitness patients to our clinic. We originally developed ourselves to be a concierge service to Dr. Baumgartner's patients with the plan to improve outcomes, and not specifically to use as a means to attract new patients to the clinic. We instantly recognized that this was the type of program that the community was seeking. The medical integration created trust and comfort for those who would not normally join a gym. We knew we could optimize our patients results with functional medicine and safely progress patients suffering from pain and degeneration. Communicating between the medical and fitness staff, we could provide the maximum safety, progression and results by integrating our care.

We faced our share of ample mistakes along the way. Countless hours were spent developing our program from scratch and exhausted an ocean of money on ineffective advertising. We set up pricing structures incorrectly, and had no continuity built in our programs. Blocks of sessions were sold rather than putting clients on automatic draft or long-term life changing programs. Truthfully, in the beginning, I was not the leader I needed to be. I've since accumulated a much greater purpose through my faith, support systems, leadership and mastermind training that Dr. Baumgartner invested by attendance.

I was always a caring and passionate leader, but I had to overcome my past communication style to become the most influential. Years of struggles with self-confidence and challenging what I perceived as unnecessary authority turned me into a person who reacted first versus seeking to understand. Much time has passed. I've grown. I have grown immensely personally as well as an organization we have discovered how to operate much more effectively. Over the past seven years, Dr. Baumgartner has spent over $275,000 in just me personally, not including what he spends on the rest of the team receiving top level business, marketing, automation, leadership and system management mentorship. I have harnessed the investment!

Years in medical school taught Dr. Baumgartner to be a great doctor. My schooling gave me a base of basic business management. Like many new adventures, we were not the most advanced when it came to building a business. Over time our model has grown following the philosophy of adding different sources of revenue to the business model once one sector is performing well. Positioning all your eggs in one basket makes you vulnerable. It's all about creating multiple streams of income and increasing the value of each patient while maximizing each patient's health outcome. There are going to be swings in the economy, this we know. Prepare yourself with a recession-proof business, so you will keep sailing no matter what happens.

With the uncertainty of the healthcare reform, it is critical that we take protective measures to ensure the success and livelihood of our practices. Devising a strong blend of cash paying services, along with insurance contracted services, is critical to your survival in today's competitive environment.

Traditionally, medical services tend to slow a little in the first month or two after the New Year due to insurance deductibles resetting. Developing multiple streams of income makes for a stable system no matter what time of the year, whether Dr. Baumgartner is seeing patients or out of the office educating and speaking engagements. Today our practice can survive all on its own with the current team we have even if Dr. Baumgartner were to remove himself from the practice.

	2009	2010	2011	2012	2013	2014	2015	2016
Total Sales(Revenue)	1,343,922.32	2,166,000.03	2,443,240.36	3,061,528.14	3,007,185.42	3,322,826.00	5,059,227.00	6,760,562.00
Fitness (Revenue)	NA	131,210.82	314,121.34	675,219.12	666,448.89	804,903.00	1,232,955.00	1,418,107.00
Fitness Referral	NA	107,890.00	206,040.45	345,678.90	392,825.00	588,220.00	928,265.68	1,169,053
Net Income	459,688.90	211,894.25	150,103.26	272,017.54	47,304.00	(225,000.00)	61,758.92	159,012.00
Net Income + Salary	569,288.90	701,469.09	566,347.76	705,597.85	387,304.00	115,000.00	401,758.00	479,000.00

In January, the Weight Loss & Performance Center netted **$50,551.75.** A potential slow month at the clinic due to deductibles resetting can still be a very lucrative month. Dr. Baumgartner could have taken the whole month off. The practice is still making an impact on the community and generating an income without the need to have the medical providers be present at all times. This also creates an environment for higher retention due to provider satisfaction when having multiple team members.

Due to the success of growing Rejuv and the education I was receiving I became the CFO and Practice Administrator after training my replacement as the Medical Fitness Director. After implementing and improving efficiencies in both the clinic and fitness facility alongside experiencing some very tough trials with staff that at times expressed I was the wrong fit due to my lack of medical background, I urged Dr. Baumgartner that it was time to share our model to the world. It was a vital decision. He was hesitant at first as it's in his nature as a physician to be a perfectionist. He did not feel comfortable selling a model when we still had gaps in certain areas in our operation.

I convinced him that perfection is nearly impossible in any clinic and we would always have continuous improvement efforts at Rejuv through Lean 6 Sigma and EOS Traction. I comforted him that this was also my baby and could never imagine myself not caring so deeply that I would allow myself to grow away from Rejuv. Stressing that our success at Rejuv is the only way I could ever confidently market this model to other physicians and that the vision we had for impacting health worldwide was for us to become leaders with this innovation.

In 2014 Dr. Baumgartner made the leap. It was time. He and I partnered in a new company called MedFit to help spread our Medical Fitness Impact Plan to the world. I became the CEO of both companies and started with four other practices nation-wide who were interested and captivated with what we created. In one of the opportunities, we established another Rejuv Medical in Tucson, AZ with Dr. John Tait. Dr. Tait was going to start a clinic with the same offerings we had in Minnesota. Another opportunity was in Chicago with a group that had a PM&R and Functional Medicine practice.

Another was a successful OBGYN physician that was not looking to grow, rather having an ancillary revenue source to help her patients with healthy labors, gestational diabetes, postpartum depression and healthy body weight composition post baby. The other a chiropractic clinic looking to grow and have preventative and fitness as a solution to healthy living offerings to make an impact in their community.

Each scenario was another level up for us presenting new challenges such as coaching other trainers and practice owners to buy-in to the same philosophies and strategies to intensify and strengthen the program. Learning and growing a deep understanding of practice management through consulting with various experts, MGMA, AAOE while having no formal medical administration training presented its own challenges. Additionally, coaching physicians to grow and follow the same growth map we have incorporated. Management, leadership and coaching is much of the same however the approaches with each group required a deep and intensive learning curve. Whether coaching and leading patients, trainers, staff, or physicians many of the same principals exist. To create change and development one must understand we each are our own limiting factor for progression, self-fulfillment and triumph.

Until we take full responsibility for our course and vision it's impossible to inspire a team for true growth. The conversions we personally craft are where the quantum leaps occur. The skills and technical components can be acquired or easily delegated once we connect with our deep reasoning with why we are doing what we are doing. We must become aware of our gaps and implement the necessary changes in ourselves and our practice to see the outcomes we desire in life. The right coaching and support will provide the strategic effectiveness and opportunities for you to fulfill your vision. Many of the people I coach have big dreams but some are not ready for the change it takes. My goal for all is the same. Tough love, conversations in identifying gaps, solution finding, strategy planning and taking massive action. I want all my clients to be an ANT (action not talk).

Not all our groups have been as successful and some have failed. I must look in the mirror first as personal accountability is a recurring assessment. We delivered way too much information without a step-by-step action plan based on where they were at when we met them. We provided everything without holding back which can be intimidating if not prepared for the intensity of the hard work ahead to be able to reap the rewards.

However, not all Implementers or physicians had the same skill set Dr. Baumgartner and I have been blessed with, were willing to put in the same work hours we did in the beginning to learn new skills or grow their practice, or spend the same way we did with marketing and staff development. In the beginning, I had difficulty having the real conversations with physicians and Implementers, nor were they willing to take full responsibility for the change necessary to grow the way we did. We thought they could all have the same success by adding the full spectrum of care the way we did from the beginning. We didn't force key performance metric reporting to see daily gaps and where customized training needed to occur. We just thought they could implement all at once the way we did. We didn't have the structure, weekly training and coaching the way we do now. We needed to deliver more structure, customization and support. Structure is the only way to achieve freedom and automation.

Once we identified the gaps in our delivery, we created our 6-step formal process, "The Medical Fitness I.M.P.A.C.T. Plan". A blueprint that guides each new clinic through the specific steps with customized coaching, support, skills training and made them part of our community. We had to adapt to create lasting change in each group so we could better serve practices who were ready to make the same impact we were providing our community. Presently, we turn away more people than we accept into the Medical Fitness Impact Plan based on our assessments and application process. If there are gaps that would prevent any chance of success, we hold on moving forward until they finish the first three pillars of the "Medically Fit Practice Success Platform" or a similar high-level business and marketing training course. Our platform consists of 5 Pillars: Personal Development, Business, Marketing, Medical Fitness and Integration. Each pillar dives deep into all the necessary components for lasting practice success. This training will provide great value for the practice and significantly increase the thriving implementation of "The Medical Fitness I.M.P.A.C.T.

Plan" to their facility. These prerequisites significantly increase one's practice success rate.

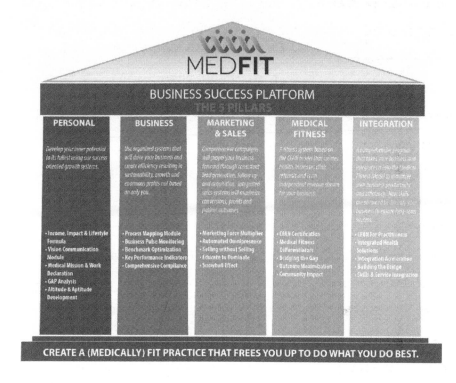

Our success to date has been due to initial sacrifice through intense and extreme working hours from Dr. Baumgartner and I, along with a TEAM that has continuously supported our mission to make an undeniable impression in healthcare. I look at how important each of those team members have been in our journey. Without several of them, their sacrifices and investment of time in our organization I would not be here writing this book.

The investment and resources dedicated to building our programs, our team and personally learning from the world's best was and will always remain a priority. Our mission and success would not have been possible without all the virtuous, brilliant and results-driven team members that we have been blessed with. We are forever indebted to our team and patients who have guided us to the place we are today.

We have made our program as turn-key as possible although to accomplish this each team member must be willing to sacrifice, change, learn, lead and invest in their team and program to make their vision come to life. Before any practice is considering this model a Discovery Call with the potential candidate consists of a comprehensive assessment to determine the most effective action steps to build the practice that can change the lives of those you serve.

Take your Medically Fit Practice Success Assessment Here: http://www.smartbizquiztribe.com/quiz/1348

Chapter 2

The 6 Step Medical Fitness I.M.P.A.C.T. Plan
How Does (I.) INTEGRATION Grow the Practice & Create Multiple Streams of Income

"Physicians sometimes tend to be cautious, so they miss out on a lot of opportunities" ~ Leigh Page, MS, Medscape (from the article *Six Ancillary Services Worth Considering*) October 15, 2012

Last year Rob our LPN/Regenerative Communication Specialist came to my office to express an exciting call he received. He is responsible for facilitating calls and conversing prospective patients through Rejuv's CFAN process to ensure we communicate our method for producing the best possible healing outcomes. He said, "John Doe called and asked what our cost was for our Bone Marrow Stem Cell Treatment." Rob's experience tells him not to jump right into prices for a few reasons. The first is we are not the "bargain price" in our area by any stretch, for any of our services, and our unique differentiating factor is not our pricing. Secondly, if we do this for any service that we offer we may not qualify that this prospective patient is a good fit for our practice without fully listening to the patient and asking the right questions.

We clearly communicate with our patients, team and business affiliates what it takes to achieve the best results, promotion, raises and success one is seeking. We have no obstacle training a patient who is just looking to get moving, as any positive change is a step in the right direction. However, the greatest results come from behavior, nutritional and mindset changes. Last, and most importantly, our value comes from Integrating all our departments to create a comprehensive approach and patient centered care.

Rob asked the patient, "do you have recent blood labs in the last six months, x-ray and MRI images so we can review your candidacy for success with our treatments?" The asked what these would be used for. Rob reply is that the "labs will determine if your cell health and hormones are in the right balance to create the proper healing environment and your images will be reviewed by Dr. Baumgartner to see if you are an appropriate candidate for this treatment. He prefers if you are close enough to receive an exam and full history evaluation first because in many instances some of our insurance covered treatments through covered injections, physical therapy, and proper eating can eliminate the need for this procedure.

For now, I would like to send you the information on our CFAN process to maximize healing outcomes and access to our Rejuv

University that has anti-inflammatory cook book, meal plans, and physician education in preparation for your office visit. Would you like to schedule for an office visit to review your labs and for a full exam so we can go over all your options?" Mr. Doe replied, "Wow! I have called several places and no one asked me these questions and review with me what it would take for me to be successful. You didn't even try to sell me your stem cell procedure and possibly cost yourself a good sale as this is what I thought I needed right away. What does next week look like for an appointment?"

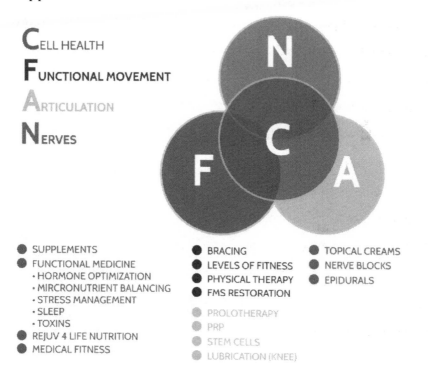

CELL HEALTH

FUNCTIONAL MOVEMENT

ARTICULATION

NERVES

- SUPPLEMENTS
- FUNCTIONAL MEDICINE
  - HORMONE OPTIMIZATION
  - MIRCRONUTRIENT BALANCING
  - STRESS MANAGEMENT
  - SLEEP
  - TOXINS
- REJUV 4 LIFE NUTRITION
- MEDICAL FITNESS

- BRACING
- LEVELS OF FITNESS
- PHYSICAL THERAPY
- FMS RESTORATION
- PROLOTHERAPY
- PRP
- STEM CELLS
- LUBRICATION (KNEE)

- TOPICAL CREAMS
- NERVE BLOCKS
- EPIDURALS

Jay Abrahams book, *Getting Everything You Can Out of All You've Got*, is one of my favorite books of all time. He talks about the principal of being Preeminent. That for you to be successful long term you must be different and a leader in what you sell or provide. He also speaks to being the leader in one of many categories to separate you from competitors. To have a Unique Selling Position (USP) that you and your team can clearly articulate to prospective patients or you will drown in a sea of mediocrity. Each patient or customer needs to be told exactly the most effective means of transformation through your services. I call it "My Mom Factor." My mom suffers from Lupus and heart disease and some chronic injuries. I would be doing my mom a great disservice to not communicate and inspire her to make an investment in each area it will take to be well-off. I want her to be around to see my kids grow and be a part of our lives as long as possible. This means explaining the need for functional medicine and specific labs, personal training, health coaching, nutritional plans, regenerative therapies, and the nutraceuticals she will need to take to get the greatest benefit from our services. Persons that do not understand these principals always consider 'well this is just asking for more money'. It's ok, this was my mentality at one point too. Our personal health is the greatest asset we have. Most people spend money on things that won't provide long-term happiness. We buy expensive vehicles, clothes, electronics, eating out, substances, gambling and fruitless entertainment that we would all trade in an instant when our body and health start to fail us. Most people I talk to state their family is their life and everything. Without health, we risk losing what is most precious to us. Prevention has always been a tough sell but I promise you that any investment now will save you ten times what it will cost you in the long run if you acquire any metabolic syndrome or autoimmune disease.

We are very sympathetic and empathetic to the patients who suffer from disease and injury. We created a model that offers hope and solutions to reverse or properly manage what we have brought upon ourselves. Don't get me wrong, not all disease or injury is self-imposed, but most of the problems stem from years of lifestyle choices, the environment and state of stress we live in, chemicals and toxins in foods, pharmaceuticals and genetics we carry. Our goal is to uncover the root causes to formulate and execute a plan of action that will prevent and reverse chronic disease and body degeneration.

Susan D. came to us shortly after I joined the practice. She had multiple joint replacements, was on seventeen medications to manage pain and could only move very gingerly. A woman with a zest for life and a personality you couldn't help but love, unfortunately was on the verge of hopelessness and despair for her future due to her state of pain.

She arrived at Rejuv after viewing an ad a local magazine highlighting our medically supervised weight loss programs. After meeting with her I knew she needed to be with Dr. Baumgartner and physical therapy before we were comfortable establishing a safe and slowly progressing training program with medical oversight for her. Susan began meeting with our functional medicine provider to optimize thyroid, testosterone, balance estrogen and progesterone and Vitamin D levels. She was also prescribed nutraceuticals such as turmeric, magnesium, and glutamine among others. She started following the Rejuv4Life meal plan eating anti-inflammatory foods.

Slowly, Christine our MFS Manager had her performing functional daily movements and began to incorporate resistance training and balance program we created and later named "Levels of Fitness Training System." In just six months' time Susan lost fifty pounds. I remember vividly her coming to me with tears in her eyes proclaiming the difference Rejuv's model made in her life. Susan expressed she had come off all but three of her medications and was re-energized with a new perspective in life. To this day she still trains with Christine as her rock and motivation to continue to live with zest and vitality. Meet Susan in the photo below (top left). We all knew at this point that we had developed the right model of healthcare. Ever since we have worked with purpose, passion and relentless persistence to multiply this model to our community and the world.

I'm going to explain what has been the most effective for us, but it does not mean you must model our formula exactly. We designed a licensing program with "The Medical Fitness Impact Plan" that can fit into any medical system. Each of the principles we've learned can help any medical practice grow its income exponentially. This model will work with any clinic or hospital system after innovating the proper integration plan. We have implemented the model as an ancillary service to increase the bottom line and patient outcomes and impact. A target/goal is imperative when starting anything new, and this was ours. When we learned how much we could aid people with this program and how motivated and ambitious our community was about our offerings it was time to take our model to yet a higher level.

After a trip to "Fitness Business Summit" we met Bedros Keuilian. After attending Bedros' summit, it was an effortless choice to invest in his mastermind to learn how to properly run a fitness business and learn how to effectively market the program. Soon after attending his first mastermind The Medical Fitness Impact Plan became our number one growth factor and USP.

Too many people looking to lose weight fear gyms, have no idea how to see results, are worried about injury, or are too high-risk to do it alone. There are millions of fad diets out there that are causing even further damage to today's population. That is why there is such great demand for a solid medically supervised program like the one we have created and have proven successes.

Medical Fitness is the finest medicine. It is not only designed to maximize patient outcomes; it became an integrated system that created an extra 1.75 million dollars in revenue to our existing sports and orthopedic practice just years later. Not every patient has a sports or orthopedic need right off the bat, relying on just injured clients to come in would have been a slow way for us to grow the practice. On the other hand, today's population has a need for exercise, proper nutrition and functional medicine optimization. Due to the obesity epidemic and the cost on society, there is a glaring emphasis on the need for a medically supervised weight loss. This program is completely different from what is offered at your local health club.

Medical fitness is easier to market than a typical medical practice. We use multiple lead generation systems, which I will cover in the upcoming chapters, that interest and motivate people to schedule a consultation. After the consultation takes place, we will recommend a program to best suit the prospects needs. Many of our patients need to start with one-on-one training that is medically supervised. This maximizes accountability and is completely individualized. Most of our one-on-one training is a cash-based program and the medical component is covered by insurance in our model. Other locations we partnered with have a goal to operate as a pure cash system.

After the initial assessment and for those who struggle to see immediate results it starts to impact the sports and orthopedic and functional medicine side of the practice. Almost all our patients with any-risk factors start with a clinical health assessment.
The office visit is typically covered through insurance if the diagnosis fits and they have risk factors requiring a pre-activity

evaluation. We do it this way as we are not an ACA state. ACA compliant states may code this appointment differently. After the lab work comes back we will determine whether the hormones need balancing or further functional medicine labs (typically not covered by insurance) are recommended based on exam. During the assessment and evaluation, if there are injuries present in addition to any metabolic concerns or diagnoses, we may recommend an orthopedic evaluation. At this time, we will also recommend that they see our physical therapist. After the physical therapist makes a treatment plan, the request is made for further insurance covered visits if necessary. All the medical services that are billed to insurance are based on recommendations in our model. For nutrition services with the dietician or health coaching the patients will use one of their training sessions for cash visits.

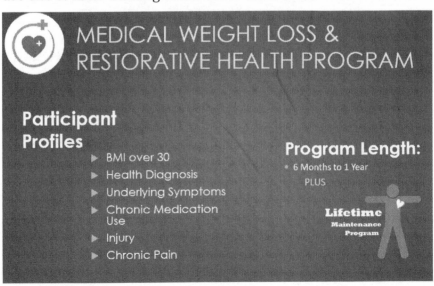

MEDICAL WEIGHT LOSS & RESTORATIVE HEALTH PROGRAM

Participant Profiles

- ► BMI over 30
- ► Health Diagnosis
- ► Underlying Symptoms
- ► Chronic Medication Use
- ► Injury
- ► Chronic Pain

Program Length:

- ● 6 Months to 1 Year

  PLUS

Lifetime
Maintenance
Program

Clinical Components

- Health Risk Assessment
  - Health History
  - Medication Review
  - Biometric Measurements
  - Comprehensive Blood Panel
- Clinical Referrals Based on Individual Need:
  - Hormone Consult
  - Orthopedics
  - Physical Therapy
  - Psychologist

- Metabolic Testing
  - What you Burn:
    - Resting Metabolic Rate
    - Lifestyle & Activity
    - Exercise
  - Weight Loss Zone
  - Maintenance Zone
- BioScore-score given based on combined factors

Internal Factors
- Total Cholesterol
- HDL
- LDL
- TC/HDL Ratio
- Triglycerides
- Glucose
- HbA1c

External Factors
- BMI
- BF%
- Waist Circumference
- Blood Pressure
- Smoking Status

In many instances after getting the medical procedures, our professionals clear the patients' physical capacity to get started or continue to work with them until they are ready to begin the medical fitness portion of our program. In turn we can better serve the patients' long term health by getting the medical care they need before getting them back to the cash-based medical fitness program with the trainers, dieticians or health coaches they initially sought out. In many cases the client may just have the metabolic test and physical, then be cleared to start with our MFS. In most instances a patient will utilize and benefit by utilizing multiple services at one time. For example, a patient may undergo rehab with a physical therapist for knee issues, but also work with a personal trainer for exercise on uninjured areas, dietician for nutrition coaching or health coach for support and accountability or behavioral phycologist for behavioral intervention and modification. Our focus is on communicating between departments regarding the best treatment program for patients when multiple providers are involved. It's a true team effort that pays off in better health outcomes for our patients! The result is less medications, less unneeded surgery, decreased weight, decreased chronic disease, improved risk factors, increased strength, greater functionality with active daily living movements, enhanced energy, a positive outlook for the future and vitality for life increases.

It is imperative to learn how to operate with ancillary services properly or consult with a lawyer in your state regarding the anti-kickback and STARK Laws. When fitness advocates meet with a high-risk patient during an initial consultation, we ask him or her to ask the patient to get clearance or a physical from their primary doctor if they decide to forgo our medically supervised program. If they do not have one, we are okay with referring the patient in-house for general services that their PCP would normally handle. There is no concern for specialty services such as sports and orthopedic injuries or cash-based medical services such as bio-identical hormones. When our medical providers refer our patients to other ancillary services as they came directly to the clinic for an injury and recommend physical therapy and/or weight loss, we must educate the patient that we have a direct ownership relationship of these entities and that they could go to several of the surrounding practices we have listed on our referral pads. This way the patient could focus on losing weight or work through their injuries on their own, but for communication purposes and the strength of our programs it is my recommendation of working within our facilities. Because each state is different, this model is one of the first things we discuss with new owners with whom I am consulting.

If a potential patient enters our facility who only wants to lose 15 pounds and is not considered to be high-risk or have any major orthopedic needs, in many instances they will go directly into personal training. During the consultation, we also have semi-private training, which is more affordable than one-on-one training, level specific boot camps such as weight loss strength and endurance, or advanced. We also have multiple transformation programs. These are the most common way to gain new patients. They are marketed programs such as our Biggest Loser Contest, 21 Day Metabolic Reset program, 20# in 42 Days, New Year's Revolution, Rock Your Skinny Jeans for The Holidays, Little Black Dress Project and the list goes on and on. We also provide online programs with many of the same services. We created an online "Rejuv University" system with medical provider videos that teaches clients everything from anatomy, basic exercise physiology, fitness and weight loss principals, nutrition, grocery store tours, and behavioral modification. The online education system is a value for patients that sets us apart from any competition. Education and understanding will increase patient compliance and outcomes of any of our services. Rejuv University has our Rejuv4Life Cookbook and meal plans. Even if a patient comes in just for injury or functional medicine we give all our patient's free access to the system to optimize outcomes even if they do not participate in one of our training programs. When other clinics invest in our Medical Fitness Impact Plan we build out the platform and brand it with their clinic's name and logo as this is our best tool and resource for reaching all our patients. Some groups have no desire to have in-house training programs and have solely purchased this platform for their clinic.

Patients who come for fitness programs end up in the clinic 62% of the time for one or more services. Some of these services, such as the metabolic testing and bio-scores, are recommended to every patient. Several of the higher reimbursing services such as pre-exercise assessments, bio-identical hormone testing and functional labs, or orthopedic services are used depending on patient needs.

In most cases, as patient's progress through their programs, they begin to know, like, and trust us. The patient will experience by observations that that we truly do have their best interests at heart and once we realize what key element is preventing them from seeing their desired results, we can make an informed recommendation for additional clinical services. At times, it can be difficult during the first session to communicate to a new fitness patient they need every service that we offer. It's a matter of time and trust before our clients and their families start seeing our medical clinic for services we offer that could benefit them. Each service we offer reflects our standards of quality care, patient centered service and a solution for optimal clinical outcomes.

Using this system, we drastically cut marketing expenses to the orthopedic practice. Almost a third of new clinical patients are derived from being introduced to the fitness programs. Just recently have we taken a greater emphasis on marketing regenerative medicine as we have had an increase in providers, successful patient transformations and an impressive number are seeking stem cells and PRP (Platelet Rich Plasma) injections.

The example form below presents some of the integrated services that we offer. During the fitness sales process, something is usually recommended from the clinical menu, and it is further down the patient experience timeline that many of the other services are utilized. For example, if a fitness patient is struggling to see change, providing trust has been established they are more open to see a medical provider to evaluate and assess labs to uncover why a patient may be wedged.

Here is an example of some of the services offered when they sign with one of our fitness programs:

Welcome to Rejuv Medical! As a new fitness or weight loss patient, there are many services available to you to help ensure your safety and reach your goals faster.

- ***Metabolic Testing** – This is a resting test that determines the number of calories you burn during basic living. It calculates the caloric requirement of the body to be awake, breathe, and digest meals. From that number, we can precisely predict the number of calories needed from exercise or dietary adjustments to maintain, lose or gain weight. This test is billable to most insurance companies. Typical deductibles/co-insurance would typically apply. It is billed with CPT code 94690. Billable cost is $128.40. If your BMI is under 30 and there are no cardiac risk factors, it can also be done without the insurance and a 33% prompt pay discount can be applied if* payment is made at time of testing. This would be a total of $86.03.

- **Pre-Exercise Assessment** – *This is a screening visit at the Rejuv Medical Clinic with either an MD or a Certified Nurse Practitioner. This exam should be performed before undergoing any strenuous training or conditioning program or intense weight loss program. This is not a "complete physical," but an examination that provides further recommendations, restrictions, and accommodations. It is not to take the place of your annual exam with your primary care provider, although aimed at screening risk factors that could be a danger to your health while performing activities that may place a higher demand on the body's systems. From this point the provider may order additional tests that may be needed. This exam is billable to most insurance companies. Typical deductibles/co-insurance would typically apply. It is billed with CPT code 99204. Billable cost is $283.00 to the insurance. Prompt pay discount can be applied if insurance is not being used. Cost with that at the time of service is $189.61.*

- **Lab Testing** – *The amount for labs and the CPT codes used is variable based on the findings from* *the provider's initial assessment. These labs are used to screen for medical factors that could affect weight loss and/or to screen for risk factors associated with obesity or high-end training. If there are questions about insurance coverage for specific labs, ask and we can get the codes for you to use to call your insurance company before having blood drawn.*

- **EKG** – *Also known as an electrocardiogram, this test uses pads on the torso, arms and legs to measure the electrical activity of the heart. It is helpful in reviewing potential heart issues. This test may be recommended based on the American Academy of Cardiology Guidelines for pre-exercise screening. It bills to the insurance company with the CPT code 93000. Billable cost is $190.00. Prompt pay discount can be applied if insurance is not being used. Cost with that payment type at the time of service is $127.30.*

- **Stress Test** – *Depends on medical referral.*

- **Dietician/Health Coaching/Behavioral Psychologist** – *Depends on type and insurance provider. Doctor referral needed. Cash option is usable at any time in replacement of a training session or at $50 for 30-minute coaching session.*

- **Physical Therapy** – *Depends on medical referral*
- **ALCAT or LEAP Food Sensitivity Testing** – *Referral needed*
- **Exercise Physiologist** – *Depends on medical referral*
- **Hormone Testing** – *Depends on insurance and labs selected*
- **Orthopedic or Sports Medicine Services** – *Joel Baumgartner MD and his team of non-surgical Orthopedic physicians use the latest technology in Regenerative Medicine and Orthopedics to get your pain, injuries or arthritis issues resolved so you can live the life you deserve. They do NOT believe in Band-Aid medicine!*

  Most of these services can be billed to your private health insurance or Medicare. Please call the insurance company (800 number is usually on the back of your insurance card) to verify Rejuv Medical/is in network and to determine your deductible amounts and your level of co-insurance or co-pay. *

The system also works vice-versa. If we are treating a patient for orthopedic needs, the providers will recommend utilization of our programs to exercise properly from a preventative standpoint once they have been cleared from physical therapy. If one of our patients is tired and fatigued from their hormones being out of balance, they can benefit from learning to eat properly and exercise. Our goal is to be the one-stop shop that is literally changing thousands of lives by steering our patients in the right direction and creating permanent changes in their health and reversing chronic disease, as opposed to a supplement store, a gym, or any other professional who doesn't have the best tools to help their patients. If a patient enters our clinic first we always provide each patient access to Rejuv University and a free medical fitness test drive for additional support, accountability, and customized guidance based off the first two evaluations.

Medical Fitness Wellness Program

How to access Rejuv University:

www.RejuvUniversity.com

Username: guest

Password: changemylife

320.217.8480 | www.RejuvMedical.com

Medical Fitness Test Drive

- 2 Week Free Pass Includes:
  - Infrared Sauna
  - Studio Classes
  - Open Gym Access
  - Educational Seminars
  - Childcare
  - Towel Service

- Health Assessment
- Functional Movement Screening
- Customized Medical Fitness Sessions

Most facilities who have implemented The Medical Fitness Impact Plan have the potential to add an additional $100,000 in revenue the first year from the fitness programs. The only requirements to start is a small room and an "Implementer," and "The Medical Fitness Impact Plan" to save time and to get it right. Knowing what we know now, you can easily duplicate our system and create profits much faster than we did when finding the right "Implementer". By aiding in this mission, you can essentially positively enhance thousands of lives, which has been our dream and vision all along.

This plan is designed to add additional patients to the practice with minimal time, overhead, investment, and risk when added the right way. The last chapters will dive deep into the way to "get it right". The best part is that it's not completely dependent on the medical provider's time. Yes, you will need either a physician, nurse practitioner, physical therapist, or chiropractor once the charge provider can no longer see additional patients, or when you are ready to sail the sea and just watch your business grow.

Chapter 3

The 6 Step Medical Fitness I.M.P.A.C.T. Plan

(M.) Marketing: The Secret Sauce for Success

A common pattern of destruction I see is that many medical practices and business owners are trying to be everything to everyone. When you do this it's difficult to create an emotional connection and response to the prospect you are trying to capture. When you cast a net that is too large your message becomes diluted and your connection suffers.

The definition of a niche is vital to embrace. This may be known as a narrowly defined market that has needs that are not being met by a mainstream product or service. Advice by experience, work to not be average to everyone, but be superior to your niche. By narrowing your niche, you can add value to society by being the best you can be for your target. If you can't be in the top percentile of what you offer its very difficult to separate your practice from competition. We believe we have the top non-surgical and medical fitness integrated clinics in the world, there for it is our obligation to market and connect with those who are in need.

At our practice and with our fitness facility we have multiple services, but we don't market all our services to everyone. For our fitness, we market directly to females ages 35-55 who want to lose weight and get healthy again. Our marketing highlights our medically integrated platform that maximizes results and safe progression. We do not market to body builders, power lifters, or children. In our boot camps, we market to women between the ages of 25-40 who want to look and feel great that are looking for a supportive community that is like a second home to them. The "Cheers of Fitness". We have athletic programs as well, but they are not the core focus although each one of our fitness offerings can be maximized using our medically integrated services, so we never lose sight of integration as our marketing differentiator. We must separate ourselves from the 100 other gyms and private studios who do not have the expertise to effectively and with education offer what we can.

With our orthopedic clinic, we educate about our CFAN process that includes nutrition and fitness that separates us from any other clinic in Minnesota. Our promise is we can help transform those who suffer from disease and degeneration while looking to avoid surgery and cover up medicines. Again, no one else at the current time has the same offerings that we do. Everyone can claim they are the best, but people are attracted to new and different because everyone will claim they are the best. What makes you stand out will be key and necessary.

You must know everything about the niche you're trying to capture. Where they eat, shop, cars they drive, where they hang out, group their associated with, their habits, motivations, dreams, incomes they earn, what type of households, where they live, problems they have, can they afford you, and what their biggest fears and desires are. You need to be able to speak to your niche in their language. What are their hot buttons that inspire action? Once you have the opportunity to speak to them, you will need to be able to relate to the target group as an understanding member, not as a foreign diplomat. Unfortunately, when many doctors try to market, speak or do social media they lose people with science. We are not trying to educate other doctors rather inspire and speak at your prospects level and transformational desire. Once you know everything about your prospect and you understand them, you can create the most effective marketing campaigns.

After defining your niche market, you will experience cost effectiveness. I wouldn't want to send out 50,000 direct mail pieces to try and capture ten new patients. Once we narrow our target market we can send out 1,000 and get the same return. So why would you want to advertise your services to a niche market over a mass market? In other words, why would you want to target a smaller segment of your community over the entire community? Simply put, it's more effective, less costly and produces better results.

Before you start burning up your cash for marketing efforts that may or may not be effective, it will be imperative that you plan your marketing strategy. The first thing that should be listed in your plan is the type and size of your niche and the marketing vehicles you will use to capture your niche.

Once you have defined your target market, it is vital to formulate a marketing plan. Too often when I start working with practices many have never have taken the time to get their marketing dialed in. Before we hired a team of experts, each Sunday night I would ask myself three very important questions.

1)What am I actively doing to get more patients each week?

2)What do I do to keep our patients, get them results, turn them into long-term patients and raving fans? Yes, I do want our patients to not need us for acute or chronic conditions if we provide great care, however all of us can benefit from long term prevention and health optimization. It is important to know the difference between a one-time patient and a long-term patient. A one-time patient is someone who bought from you for one time or on a short-term solution. A long-term patient is someone under your care and protection. It's a relationship that goes beyond a single transaction. Most practices I start with have no idea of the life cycle of a patient, the average visits per referral, average monetary value per patient making it very difficult to understand what to spend to attract new patients.

3)What value can I add to my circle of influence, patients, team, family, friends, community and affiliates? We must get results or add value to people we are in relationships with. I call this relationship marketing which is far more effective, affordable and is how you build a tribe of raving fans who refer their circle of influence to you. Its why we are where we are today and less about how well or how much we have spent in marketing.

After you understand these three concepts you can dive into formulating your plan, but without the preceding your attempts will fall short of the potential value and benefit you can add to society. If your product or service adds value to society, you are doing the public a disservice by not learning how to market ethically and effectively.

There are seven key factors to setting up your marketing plan successfully:

1) Find, define and dominate your niche. Typically, successful practice owners view themselves as a specialist and not a generalist. Niche yourself down. Become the expert. Go narrow and deep with a mindset to dominate!

2) Figure out what your USP (unique selling purpose) is; Why you instead of someone else? Think about all the alternatives that people have for medical services in your community. Why should they choose you and not your competitor? What makes you unique, different and better? How can you communicate that message in your marketing that is a derivative of the transformation you are providing? We call this what is in it for them and not what you offer. What visuals can you create so your process makes sense to your team, patients and prospects?

3) Become the local celebrity and face of your practice by telling YOUR story. Everyone has a story and your story is unique to you. Most physicians don't tell their personal story and reason for doing what they do. The personal story can be relatable and is what will attract and allow people to connect with your mission more than any other marking factor.

4) Systematize everything! Have a step by step process so that your business can run without you being in it. The most successful practices have owners or team members who work on the business and not just in it. This is the only way you can create time freedom and replicate how you provide services and your plan must be well documented, communicated and practiced by all.

5) Utilize Facebook, YouTube, Snapchat, Instagram, Twitter, e-mail and website to market your practice differently than everyone else. Regular live videos multiple times a week and give your community a "peek" into the operations, the community that you've built and the patient results that you've delivered. Too many medical professionals are complaining about people getting rich in the online medical industry pushing out what they consider bad content, meanwhile they themselves are

producing zero content. Almost as bad, they are communicating content that only appeals to other medical professionals and not the actual prospective patients. Blasting great content on today's social media/online space is the fastest way to build the KNOW, LIKE and TRUST factor.

6) Once you drive traffic and leads to your website it must be able to communicate your transformation, educate, entertain, provide social proof and ultimately capture people who visit so you can start nurturing the leads. Too many people give up after the first visit or follow-up, but if you stay in front of people with great content you will meet their needs when the time is right for them. Follow up digitally and on the phone, relentlessly for maximum success. No, I'm not talking about calling people if they tell you to stop. I'm talking about caring more than they do at the present moment in time until they are ready to commit to change.

7) Culture + community + results = the "magic" potion of your business. And the "magic" potion is what leads to patients becoming raving fans who are referral giving machines. Your job is to make your patients and team evangelical about your product and service so that they

tell everyone about you! This does not happen overnight but can be executed with the right long-term strategy.

Here are three factors to have in place before investing in your marketing plan:

1) How much should you spend on marketing?

This depends if you are already established or just beginning your business. Your advertising budget should fall somewhere between 3-9% of your gross revenue. In my first years of starting the fitness side of the practice, the budget was around 15%. We lacked any formal marketing plan. I was throwing out tons of money, not tracking return, and was still waiting for prospects to come in. While we were able to gain some traffic, we over spent in many areas.

2) How are you going to track your return on investment?

At a minimum you should get a 2 to 1 return on investment on all your marketing dollars. Today I require nearly a 3-to-1 ratio on our paid marketing pieces to continue the ad spend. If it is short of this return I know something needs to be changed, such as the message, the headline, the funnel, offer or the advertising medium. For this reason, it is important to test and track your results. You can test two separate direct mail pieces to a small sample of your target market and see what piece gets you the most leads. You can use two different phone numbers to track the results. Use two different Facebook ads to the same program to see which one generates better results.

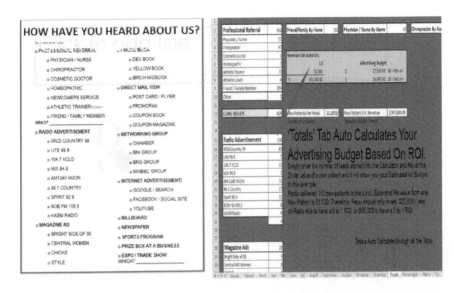

3) Marketing is just one piece of the advanced picture when it comes to getting new patients. Simply put, marketing attracts leads to your business and to express interest. For many practices, they can generate leads, but the next step is what to do with those leads once you receive them. Unfortunately, too many critical leads get lost in the mix and there is very little, if any, follow up. If this is the case you're lacking a lead nurturing system. We will dive deeper on this section in the Automation Chapter.

Having multiple marketing funnels will spread your message and may connect with someone who may not have received it in another medium. Personally, I may be a great prospect for a company, but I would never find their ad in a newspaper or on television because I don't read the news or watch TV. The prospect might hear a radio ad, see you in the newspaper, have a friend who uses your service, but it was the direct mail piece that got them in. That's called the force multipliers of marketing. For this reason, it's difficult to get a 100% accurate results in tracking one medium, but all your messages can be used together to leverage your results.

Month	January			
Week	1st	2nd	3rd	4th
Trends	College Students Return, Cold Weather	Snow Sports, Ice Man Events	Martin Luther King	
Email Marketing				
Radio				
Press Release				
Video Post				
SEO				
Social Media				
Blog Post				
Web Develop				
Direct Mail				
Joint Ventures				
Events				
Trade Shows				

In my experience, it will be one message that finally brings the prospect to you. The simply check boxes that are selected on your intake form are giving you your greatest return on investment. If you're not tracking or testing, it's imperative that you start now if you would like to make the most of your money.

Most practices and businesses will run newspaper ads, print flyers, pay per click campaigns, radio spots, and create websites that all cost loads of money. Some, completely fail to get a 2-to-1 return on investment in these high cost mediums. This is exactly how we started, but today I will discontinue any medium that isn't providing a 2 to 1 return. Another mistake practices make is by not investing more when they are getting a return. If I stick two dollars in an ATM machine and four dollars come out I would keep pumping money into it. I'm going back to that ATM repeatedly.

Initially, many practices we work with wonder why their advertising and marketing campaigns are unsuccessful at bringing in the amount of traffic one would expect. I learned that the key to marketing is to get the maximum number of prospects to KNOW, LIKE, and TRUST you. Once consumers hold you in this regard you have more people willing to trade their money for your services than you would have ever dreamed. Before you start blasting out these paid print ads, you must first start the free and most effective methods for creating likeability and trust. Many successful individuals I have spoken with feel that traditional marketing has passed its time and the key for most local practices is relationship marketing. Our focus has dramatically changed to any medium that allows us to provide content and connect with our prospects.

We still pay for radio, but only as the medical and fitness expert on radio stations, or with celebrity endorsements that have had great results with our regenerative services. On the show, we provide value by offering advice on how to make healthy changes, talk of fears, desires, hope, myths and our story and close by leading them to our website.

Too many practices are trying to brand themselves like they are McDonalds™ or Coke™. Many are looking only where everybody else is marketing and doing the same types of ads, and in the same places. "Oh my competition is in this magazine; I have to be too." To stand out today, most of your marketing dollars should be spent while building a relationship with your community and current patient base. This type of marketing will lead you to be the go-to source in your region.

Four months after opening the standalone location, we wondered why we were still losing money. This is when Dr.

Baumgartner and I went to Bedros Keuillian's Fitness Business Summit. After a weeklong conference and masses of great information, I decided to join his mastermind program. For the last 6 years now we've invested over $275,000 in mastermind programs to learn to dial in our marketing, systems, communication management and leadership skills. These have been the best financial decision we could have made. Without the help and guidance of successful business owners themselves, it would've taken many years of financial struggle along with trial and error, likely intense trial. I'm not sure we would have survived through our trying years without the support and systems we have received from each coach and consultant.

Most of our advertising dollars were going to high-cost print ads, magazines, radio stations, and billboards. Don't get me wrong, some of those avenues may fit although we found some of the most effective advertising is mostly free. Out of all our paid advertisements, only radio was providing a return on investment. We trained a well-known local DJ who lost 75 pounds in eight months on our program. She spoke and blogged of her experience on the radio. It was very successful at providing a ton of new leads. If you're looking to utilize paid advertising, this is one method I'd strongly guide you towards.

Because of the great success we had with radio, we tried the same with other DJs. But after two or three months they would fizzle out and not get long-lasting results. They simply liked the free training. Realizing it wasn't good for us, we had to come up with a different system for celebrity endorsements. Now we will take on new endorsement deals but they must successfully complete six months of training or see clinical success before we decide to do any advertising with them.

At the time, I couldn't understand why all our other marketing didn't have the same return on investment as radio. Within months of the mastermind coaching program, we quickly began to realize that we were just selling features of our program and not the transformation we help create, benefits to the person or the story behind our care. Our ads would have information such as: "We provide metabolic testing," "The program is medically supervised by a doctor," "We do grocery shopping tours, cooking classes, bio-identical hormones and regenerative procedures." As we mentioned earlier in the chapter, you can't be everything to everyone without a defined story board. Remembering this one rule will leave a meaningful impression and set the necessary tone: any marketing or content piece must state the transformation offer your service or product provides.

Several businesses spend an astronomical amount of money on fancy websites that have a generous amount of information and look pretty. That's great, but typically they are not successful because they are not pushing emotional hot buttons, they don't have an irresistible offer, social proof and they fail to call the prospect to action through education and nurturing sequences. That's great that you can help everyone, and you have three degrees, and six different programs, and you have the best equipment. Logic would say you need all that, but the reality is that people are seeking you for a pain they want solved. They want solutions, not science and information. Most medical practices with successful advertising and marketing are using the "star, story, solution" method along with social media and e-mail marketing. You will market your clinic in this regard, but with your medical fitness practice, you will use the eight important elements listed below in all your print and audio campaigns. This type of marketing is called "direct response marketing." With the eight elements below, they are led to a clearly defined desired action.

1) The headline - You must capture the attention of the audience

2) An irresistible offer - This is what a prospect will get for taking action

3) The science or reason behind your irresistible offer

4) Your USP (Unique Selling Position) – 30-day money back guarantee or medical fitness—something that separates you from all the rest

5) Social proof - The greater testimonials/case studies you have, the better

6) Create scarcity or urgency that leads the prospect to immediate action

7) The bullet points of benefits and transformation they will get from your offer

8) A strong call to action with clear directions on what you want the prospect to do next – Whether it be to go to your web page, call to sign up for a seminar, consultation or office visit, or trail period

Here is an example:

1) The headline - you must capture the attention of the audience

   - Lose 20 pounds in 42 days - free weight loss challenge

2) An irresistible offer - this is what a prospect will get for taking action.

- Normally $199, but yours for free when successfully completing the challenge

3) The science or reason behind your irresistible offer.

- This program is exchange of you sharing your story so we can help more people who can benefit from a medically integrated program

4) Your USP (Unique Selling Position) - something that separates you or your service offering from all the rest.

- The only medically supervised program in the area with medically integrated service to maximize your transformation and progress you safely based on your internal and external bio-score.

- Medically tested and proven methods to help lose weight the right way.

5) Social proof - the greater testimonials/case studies you have, the better.

- Look at these residents' before and after pictures.

6) Creating scarcity or urgency that leads the prospect to immediate action.

- We are only accepting the first 20 applicants.

7) The bullet points of benefits they will get from your offer.

- Not only will you lose weight and have more energy, you will get a done-for-you meal plan and tools that saves you thought and time.

- Discover the secrets of your metabolism and why your past diet and exercise plans have been failing you.

8) A strong call to action with clear directions on what to do.

- Enter your e-mail in the box and reserve your spot for the orientation today, offer ends 6/1/2017.

Making Your Marketing Efforts Work:

There are multiple types of marketing and advertising mediums that we could put our focus on. Whether it's paid or free marketing and advertising, you need several different funnels to best reach your target market. Each medium can bring you more leads and prospects. More leads equal more patients when you have your back-end automation in place. Each one of your mediums must have purpose and be strategically used and measured to determine effectiveness. Focus on relationship and content marketing digitally before investing into traditional and paid advertising mediums. Many businesses start Investing all their efforts in paid advertisements before researching the overlooked, more important, more effective, and much more affordable relationship and content marketing strategies. This is because every advertiser you sit in front of will tell you how their medium is perfect for you and that you will miss out if you don't take advantage of their service. It's also done for you and requires no work.

Print marketers pray you'll just hand over money and accept the first idea they come up with so they can move on to finding more business. They also hope you don't track your efforts because they can make practical sense of your dollars instead of using true data. They will make claims that your competitors are there and that it works great. If you are not obtaining an impressive return, they will tell you it takes time and you should add to your frequency. As you are paying for advertising, I ask you to consider hiring an in-house marketing and sales manager to spend all their efforts on tracking, making compelling copy, creating new business, growing community relationships and free content marketing opportunities before paying for any outside advertising.

The goal is to create as many force multipliers as possible. We do this by having several effective marketing funnels all working to get our marketing message to our target market.

Many people fail to determine whether their marketing is successful because they lack a system, the staff support to do so, or do not know how simple it can truly be, honestly there is not much to it.

What this chapter is about is stepping outside your comfort zone and not attempting an easy road. Off line marketing can take work, but it's by far the most important of all the marketing strategies to build your relationship in the community. It's easy to have the newspaper and radio craft you an ad and you're done. Not only will that probably be the least effective, it's also the most expensive. You must do the free stuff and that involves getting out in the community including but not limited to speaking, writing and video content every chance you get, social media, joint ventures, chamber meetings, grocery store tours, referral generation systems, and transformation contests.

The online marketing and paid tools can be extremely effective as well, but I have seen many owners and managers get too comfortable sitting behind the computer. Funnels like Facebook, SEO, Pay Per Click, Craig's List, e-mail marketing, and having an effective website are significant to your success. The key is finding models that will work for you. Take the time to make a system or follow ours so you're not running around doing everything half- heartedly. You need to combine both online and offline, free and paid advertising, and pump money into the things that work well for you at building relationships and building trust. This is the long-term approach that needs time and resources invested into it to make it work.

No matter what funnel you use your marketing message must explain why your practice exists and share your story. It's a crowded marketplace and you need a reason for people to want to be part of your cause. Your message needs to speak to the prospect. If they know your "why," it will be easy to build a relationship with your prospects and patients. As a medical fitness facility and a medical practice, this is an easy avenue to become incredibly successful not only financially, but in your ability to change lives for the better. Your practice will be a commodity if you fail to build strong relationships with your team, patients, and prospects. If you become a commodity, then you're forced to compete on price and that's the race to failure.

Once people know your "why" and know you are invested into building relationships, the best marketing will come in the form of content. Not only will you be doing what your competitors are not, but content marketing is a marketing technique of creating and distributing relevant and valuable content to attract, acquire, and engage a clearly defined and understood target audience. Basically, content marketing is the art of communicating with your customers and prospects without selling. It is non-intrusive marketing. Instead of pitching and hard-selling your products or services, you are delivering information that makes your prospect more intelligent.

The essence of this content strategy is the belief that if we as businesses deliver consistent, ongoing, valuable information to prospects, they ultimately reward us with their business and loyalty. Consumers have simply shut off the traditional world of marketing.

Today, prospects own DVRs to skip television advertising, often ignore magazine and newspaper advertising, stream music online or listen to Pandora, and now have become so proficient at online "surfing" that they can take in online information without a care for pop-ups, banners, or buttons. In today's society, traditional marketing is just not the way to be successful and I believe this has been proven. The good thing is that you can save a lot of money by not falling victim to traditional forms of advertising.

You can create marketing content that is anticipated and truly makes a connection! You can develop and execute "sales" messages that are needed, even requested, by your prospects.

Content marketing is a distant memory from the "in your face" marketing we are smeared with every minute of every day. Content marketing is for the present and the future.

This is a powerful message and is vital to clearly define. I do not recommend hiding behind the computer to create content. Instead, most of your time should be spent on "Why Marketing" (mission) and "Relationship Marketing" (connections). You can easily outsource most of the "Content Creation" (advice and information story-telling) to copywriters, and funnel building and automation experts if you don't have time. I love to write and speak so it is not a barrier for me although making it a daily priority is a constant time management necessity. Any time I have fallen off from fighting fires and getting too deep into the day to day or growth takes a back seat.

In order to make all the multiple funnels work, it's crucial to use the marketing calendar presented earlier. It has all the mediums at the top and makes sure you are effectively planning and making your efforts work together. The difference between acting early versus reacting is critical to the implementation and success of all your efforts.

When you accomplished this, you will have more opportunities for a sale, promotion, or event. One should be thinking about January at the end of October, or proven time and time again, you will be too late.

Take the Medically Fit Practice Success Assessment to gauge where you stack up in your marketing efforts.

Take your Medically Fit Practice Success Assessment Here: http://www.smartbizquiztribe.com/quiz/1348:

Chapter 4

The Six Step Medical Fitness I.M.P.A.C.T. Plan

(P.) Personal & Personnel: The Driving Force of Practice Success

Rather than asking why so many small businesses fail, we will find more value in defining what it is that makes the top businesses in America so successful. One thing is very certain, it's not luck. The success begins with the owner and their abilities. From there, successful business must have a clear structure and leadership chain throughout the organization. This was something that our own organization was delayed in positioning even as critical as those two components are. By trial and error, it became crystal clear the two primary components were required and until we conformed it caused numerous problems on multiple levels. It has not been the effort of one person that has built a winning practice, but a collaboration of many team members working together for a common goal.

There is a formula for everything in the business world and every successful business has their own unique ingredients. You have every single capability the successful businesses have and recognizing that is an important key to realizing the dream can happen. In fact, you've got better access to information today than many ultra-successful people and businesses do. You don't have to reinvent the wheel but most owners and managers must grow as leaders to have a winning formula. Follow the footsteps of some of the most persistent, hard-working, and passionate leaders and companies in the world. I make sure to surround myself with successful people. A few traits they have acquired remain common among all of them: the courage of a lion, a healthy mindset and ability to lead or inspire followers.

It takes heart to realize that you deserve more, to step outside your comfort zone, to be willing to do whatever it takes, to make decisions that others won't, have the conversations that need to be had, be willing to take risks, deal with fear and uncertainty and to take daily action.

But I can't provide you with heart. I cannot force you to be an action taker, instill work ethic or force you to grow as a person. What I can give you is access to the tools, tactics, resources, action steps, systems, strategies, ideas and inspiration to make you and your medical fitness practice a colossal success. Once you are overcome with the passion to do what it takes, the next step is making sure you have the right mindset for success. Unlike heart, you can be taught to acquire the right mindset. Leadership and proper communication takes courage and practice, but anyone can learn these skills, I'm living proof.

Do you have the right mindset to be successful? Is there logic for every decision that is made? Mindset means doing everything to make your dreams and vision a reality and knowing you can make it happen. When you have the right mindset, you can weed out anything that is not fitting in with your core values of making your vision come to life. Will you do everything it takes? There is no plan B approach philosophy. Do you have a mind of abundance or scarcity? Will there be enough patients for you to help and there is no competition that can stop you if you do what you do best and have control of? Do you fully understand that you are the only thing that stands in your way of success? That it's not the economy, our current medical system or lack of capable people to help you? Do you believe without a shadow of a doubt you can be successful and were born to have a lasting impact? You must think like a champion to be a champion.

I have removed myself from all the negativity, drama and limited thinking that had previously prevented me from moving forward in my early years. You must surround your staff and yourself with pure positivity and forward thinking. Many entrepreneurs don't have what it takes mentally to survive the business world. They're limited in belief; the glass ceiling that stops them from reaching their full potential. It is our opinions and thoughts that get in the way of being truly successful in life. What I've learned is how to separate fact from fiction, our opinions and beliefs from facts, and how to truly get over any mental hurdles that stand in our way. That is how we coach many entrepreneurs. You can truly make your income and impact exponential instead of linear if you learn how to acquire the right mindset.

In one of my very first coaching masterminds I was told to buy the audio of *The New Version of Psycho Cybernetics* by Max Maxwell. It was instrumental in preparing me for success in our practice. When taking new leaps, such as with this program, we are always faced with fear and doubt. Again, those are just opinions versus facts. We must learn to embrace our dreams, passions, and visions into our mind with a clear-cut path on how to obtain and execute. Likely you have heard of goal setting, and that will be a big part of getting this program started.

Oftentimes, entrepreneurs do not understand their gaps or their weakness. They fail to hire people around them to do to what they can't or their ego is too big for them to change how they are perceived or operate. Low self-awareness or asking yes people versus true introspection or listening to someone who will give you truthful dialog of your blind spots. The vision in our success lies in what we must change personally and who we surround ourselves with that are better than us in our weaknesses. To be successful, harness a team that is productive and passionate in their area of genius. need a team of people working in their area of genius.

Investing time and money into resources that will educate yourself and your team to grow your practice will be a requirement. I will always pay for high level coaching until I have learned what I need from that expert and move to the next person that can continue to move me forward with even more know-how. Because you don't know what you don't know. If you think you know it all, you will have an eventual barrier to success. This is something you should do for yourself and for your team. I spend an hour each day educating myself with new books, audio, or webinars. Below are some of the important books that I have read to help me learn many of the essential tools to build a successful medical practice and licensing and consulting business. Thirty minutes are set aside to read cutting-edge medical resources and journals to help grow my business skills. The other thirty each day is for learning how to be a better person and leader. Here are some of the more important business books that will help accelerate you and your employees' learning curves. I often request that my team read some of the books directly associated with their position. I ask my Assistant Sales Manager to read all the best sales-related books and audio. This way they learn to become an expert in their position and we have acquired the same content for ease of relating. The below are my favorite books that I found worth reading and should be added to your business library. Don't feel as though you must do this all at one time. Read one book before moving on to the next.

- *E-Myth* - Michael Gerber
- *Getting Everything Out of All You Got* - Jay Abraham
- *Mastermind Marketing System* - Jay Abraham
- *Turning Pro* – Steven Pressfield
- *Awaken the Giant Within* - Anthony Robbins
- *Psycho Cybernetics* - Dan Kennedy/Max Maxwell
- *Start with Why* – Simon Sinek
- *From Good to Great* – Jim Collins
- *Traction*-Gino Wickman
- *How to be a Great Boss*- Gino Wickman
- *The Secret* – Rhonda Byrne
- *Customer Satisfaction is Worthless; Customer Loyalty is Priceless* - Jeffrey Gitomer
- *Think and Grow Rich* - Napoleon Hill
- *How to Win Friends and Influence People* - Dale Carnegie
- *Yes, Attitude* – Jeffrey Gitomer
- *The Psychology of Selling Program* - Brian Tracy
- *Delivering Happiness* – Tony Hsieh
- *Built to Last* - Jim Collins
- *The Seven Habits of Highly Effective People* - Stephen Covey
- *The Art of Closing Any Deal* - James Pickens
- *Creativity, Inc.* - Ed Catmull
- *The Soul of Leadership* - Deepak Chopra
- *Pure Genius* – Dan Sullivan
- *Ultimate Sales Letter* - Dan Kennedy

- *Killing Sacred Cows* - Garrett Gunderson
- *How to Master the Art of Selling* - Tom Hopkins
- *Low Profile Selling* - Tom Hopkins
- *Influence* - Robert Cialdini
- *Multiple Streams of Income* - Robert G. Allen
- *Cracking the Millionaire Code* - Robert G. Allen
- *The Tipping Point* - Malcolm Gladwell
- *No B.S. Local Grass Root Marketing* - Dan Kennedy
- *The Go Giver* - Bob Burg/John David Mann
- *How to Develop Self-Confidence & Influence People by Public Speaking* – Dale Carnegie
- *Making a Habit of Success* - Mack Douglas
- *Feel the Fear and Do It Anyway* - Susan Jeffers
- *The Energy Bus* – Jon Gordon
- *The Automatic Millionaire* - David Bach
- *The 5 Temptations of a CEO* – Patrick Lencioni
- *Ready, Fire, Aim* - Michael Masterson
- *Grouped* - Paul Adams
- *Richest Man in Babylon* - George S. Clason
- *SEO for 2012* - Sean Odom/Lynell Allison
- *Emotional Intelligence* - Daniel Goleman
- *The Innovators Dilemma* – Clayton Christensen
- *No B.S. Marketing to the Affluent* - Dan Kennedy
- *The Art of Strategy* - Avinash Dixit
- *Secrets of the Millionaire Mind* - T. Harv Eker
- *21 Irrefutable Laws of Leadership* - John C Maxwell
- *Competing for the Future* - Gary Hamel and C.K. Prahalad
- *How to Speak Like A Pro* - Leon Fletcher
- *The Art of Selling Fitness* – Bedros Keuilian
- *Flirting for Success* - Jill Spiegel
- *6 Sigma* - Neil DeCarlo

- *The Ultimate Blueprint for an Insanely Successful Business* - Keith Cunningham
- *Predictably Irrational* - Dan Ariley
- *Fitness Launch Formula* – Brian Devlin
- *The Carrot Principle* - Adrian Gostick/Chester Elton
- *Jack Straight from The Gut* – Jack Welch
- *Kiss That Frog* - Brian Tracy
- *The $100 Startup* - Chris Guillebeau
- *Results That Last* – Quint Studer
- *Triggers* – Marshall Goldsmith
- *Love Yourself Like Your Life Depends on It* - Kamal Ravikant
- *No B.S. Ruthless Management of People and Profits* - Dan Kennedy
- *Teaching to Change Lives* – Dr. Howard Hendricks
- *Alchemist* - Paulo Coelho
- *Expert Answers 95 Practice Management Questions* – Mary Mourar
- *Change Your Brain, Change Your Life* - Daniel G. Amen
- *The Entrepreneurial Crisis* – Erik Rokeach
- *Flow* - Michaly Csikszentmihaly
- *Positive Psychology Coaching* - Robert Biswas-Diener
- *The 22 Immutable Laws of Marketing* - Al Ries/Jack Trout
- *The Man in The Mirror* – Patrick Morley
- *The Strangest Secret* - Earl Nightingale
- *The 5 Dysfunctions of a Team* - Patrick Lencioni
- *The 10x Rule* – Grant Cardone

Acquiring the dream will demand your employees' diligent commitment and passion alongside digging their heals in and taking personal accountability for their action items. Each day you can improve your practice and be the leader in your niche. It is extremely important that all the employees have the right mindset and buy into your vision from the start. Wrong team, no dream.

You and your team's ability to lead and develop the practice is the driving force of your success. When you put in the right process to help grow your team and determine if they are right for the job you hired them to do you will achieve success much faster. It all starts with how you interview, having clear job descriptions, clear expectations and metrics for tracking success. Frequent meetings in the beginning providing feedback on performance and giving training to become better, and amazing two-way and team communication. You may have heard people don't leave their jobs they leave their managers. I'm not talking micromanagement. I'm talking about creating a culture of excellence, accountability and growth potential when it is the right fit. Team members who are versatile in times of change and resilient in times of unknown. These are necessary essentials to create a winning team. Everyone needs leadership, management and development including myself. Even as the CEO I pay experts to help me stay accountable for the goals we set. I need someone to show me ways to improve production, provide coaching and guidance while seeing me through new levels of growth while helping me avoid traps and blind-spots I might not see from my perspective.

This also makes the hiring, managing, and termination process much more vigilant and comfortable to incorporate. Some people will be the wrong fit. Gino Wickman states each person must "get it, want it, and have the capacity" for the position hired. If you continue to retain a negative attitude, a poor performer, someone who is truly not bought in or resistant to change and growth, it will not only hurt your business performance, other team members will question the leadership and accountability in your organization. You risk losing good people due to poor management and leadership. At times this does not equal retention, instead it equals right person right seat, are they right for the overall culture.

If there is one thing I have learned, it is that you must hire slow, term fast, and cut out any cancer immediately. I have had to learn this the hard way far too many times. The one challenge I still face today is some people have great value for the organization but do not fit the greatest in a team environment or at times have inflated egos therefore not fitting a core value of being virtuous. As a key leader, we are faced with asking ourselves if we develop this person because they have obvious skills, do we find better team fits, or do we carefully navigate the team to learn to better accept those that have unique skills even though they may be more rough around the edges. At this point I think it may be hard with 90 plus people to all work in perfect harmony so I continue to focus on development of all. It presents a challenge when wearing multiple hats to ensure the growth of many. Back to my point, you are only as strong as developing leaders who can develop other leaders.

This is a business and there must be clear expectations set forth from day one that we will be a place of clear process, communication, positivity, forward thinking and truly being virtuous and resilient to change. By explaining from the onset if there is anything that varies from the same system and vision that we have, it will not be tolerated. They can come to us if they believe there is a better way of operating and we will be all ears as we invite healthy disagreement and positive changes to our operations. In a medical environment, a team's ability to adapt and work together through changes is a major factor in sustainability. After a decision has been made for the greater good we all need to be on the same page and present buy-in, even if ultimately in question. If a leader shows uncertainty or expresses question, the trust in the leadership team will be in question by all. Create the buy-in, and let the team know we will get it wrong at times, and course correcting is normal if a plan has fell short of its objective.

Trust your intuition and make decisions that only correlate with your goals and visions and the core values you have put in place. Setting core values is not something to hang on the wall and walk away. Truly harnessing the core values and presenting yourself and holding others accountable is something that cannot be overlooked as this creates your culture, which will reflect in retention efforts. When there are systems in place combined with a positive atmosphere, everyone will be energized and ready to work. This is achieved when staff and the community have bought into your mission. Your happiness and fulfillment will attract greatness. Everybody wants to be a part of something as extraordinary as your practice can be.

Seek qualified employees who have the "it factor." They are out there; you just must know how to find them. It is important when you find great employees that you have systems in place to retain them as you would patients. Motivate your employees both financially and with recognition. Believe it or not, recognition holds greater value than money. When creating your medical fitness facility, you need a solid plan of attack. One of the most important reads that helped our practice succeed was *E-Myth* by Michael Gerber.

The emphasis of the book is centered on creating solid organizational systems that allow you to grow the smartest way possible. All your positions in the company must have clearly defined roles and objectives. Once you have grown to a size that requires the next position needed, you will have clearly defined objectives for that position. He defines three clear roles: the technician, manager, and entrepreneur. When starting, you may have to take on all the responsibilities of each position, but each has very clear roles and needs. Oftentimes small businesses fail because of the lack of movement or application from one role to the other.

Each subsequent move will allow you to spend more time on growing the practice. You may have to do many of the duties of the technician before you can effectively delegate to the next key addition to your organization. Some people can't move to the next stage because they can't let go and feel they must control everything. Therefore, you must create easy-to-follow systems with checks and balances. You will not be able to run your practice on your own if you are to aspire to higher income levels and help more people.

My role upon hired was to build our medical fitness program. We call the initial Medical Fitness Coordinator responsible for growing the program an "Implementer." I was able to join forces to successfully formulate the Medical Fitness Impact Plan. Dr. Baumgartner needed to be seeing patients daily. He would have lacked the time to build his practice alone. It was simple math for him to understand he had to delegate all tasks that don't have a $500 per hour value that he could generate for the practice. This is one of the most important rules you must learn to live by. Living by this rule with each subsequent hire as we learn to manage, motive, delegate, educate and let go will be vital. With Dr. Baumgartner understanding this principal he could be minimally involved in the day to day. He has enjoyed watching his team create a system that allowed for the growth of his practice and at the same time, improved thousands of lives. We constructed the medical fitness center he had a vision for without him working inside of it.

If you follow the steps in this book, you and your key startup fitness "Implementer" will take massive action to build the practice of your dreams. From what we learned, created, trialed and optimized all the "done for you" systems that have already been proven to work. The great part is that you get to skip all those painful learning lessons and take off on the right foot. Our trial and error is your win!

Who Will Run Your Medical Fitness Facility as You Grow?
Fitness Coordinator/Director, Trainers, Assistant Managers,

Administrative Assistant, Front Desk, Customer Service Manager
The role of the Fitness Coordinator/Director "Implementer" is one of the most crucial positions in the entire organization. The "Implementer" is directly responsible for the success and growth of your company's program in the starting phase. They must have the ability to acquire sales in a respectful manner. They must be passionate about helping others, able to speak to people, follow the systems in place, and having the successful ability to lead patients and employees by example.

The role of the Implementer will change as the business grows as this person will wear many hats initially. When the patient base starts to grow, the Implementer will then hire MFS to work with the incoming patients.

Your trainers will be your technicians. Their primary focus is to work with the patients and help them see results. Your Implementer will start seeing less and less patients as he or she begins filling up the trainers' schedules to work with new patients. The important part is that they understand and advance your philosophies and visions from the start. They need to follow all the systems such as your nutrition and workout programs, client retention systems, policies and procedures and integrate new fitness patients into the clinic for optimal results. Once there are two to three filled trainers, it will be time to bring on an assistant manager or back office administrator. This employee will take over many of the administrative duties the Implementer had to do. This will include billing, payroll, customer service, content delivery, and some training as well.

As growth continues, there will be a need for additional hires who specialize in specific roles that will help take your program to the next level. It can be difficult to know up front the exact hire needs because each hire has different unique skills. The goal is to find people who are better than you in different areas of need and keeping each team member working in their area of genius so they continue to be motivated. Each one of these positions has a detailed list of duties that are required to be accomplished daily. The Implementer simply inspects each employee's checklists to ensure the job is being done the right way and then will follow up periodically as needed to ensure systems and protocol are followed or possible even a system enhancement known as continuous improvement.

There is a system for when the next key employee is needed. The Implementers role will be to implement all the systems. As growth allows, the position evolves to where the sole focus is managing systems, motivating, developing content, delegating, and selling. The goal is to delegate all essential duties required to run the facility so you can focus on growth outside the facility. In two years and six months, I was done working daily in the fitness center and moved to CFO/Vice President position that oversees the entire clinic/fitness operation. I was responsible for overseeing both the clinic and the fitness facility operations. My role as CFO/VP consisted of overseeing the entire workforce for Dr. Baumgartner, developing documented systems, inspecting all of these once in operation and making hundreds of changes along the way to get a much more effective, scalable, and profitable organization. It started by finding out just what our processes were, what everyone was doing, what our numbers looked like. The team helped me create and pull together financial tracking systems that finally let us learn all the metrics behind our business. Phase I was to make our practice completely systemized and automated. There have been several adaptations and improvements from the initial system out of necessity as we grew. New EHR two times, integrated technology, different roles, new additions and you name it, we crossed each one.

Trust me, trying to get everyone on the same page, especially from some guy who had no clinical experience was no easy task. We have lost good talent while we have gained even more amazing team members all who have helped get us to where we are today. In our time, we have had different personalities, views, individual visions, wrong people in wrong seats. We have had the right people, in the wrong seat. You name it, we have learned and lived through some tough failures and mistakes. We have lost insurance contracts for performing outside the box treatments. We have lost focus at times by doing too many projects at once. There have been hard times and amazing times and we will not stop short of aiding in the mission to restore health worldwide. Building something of this nature has been the more prevalent and rewarding challenge Dr. Baumgartner and I have ever had.

Two peers that I worked with told me I was going to have my hands full and that I was taking an impossible position which I already knew. Although I also knew from my past I have always been born with a never quit mentality and withstand the greatest trials. I knew from the beginning we were going to change healthcare with this model and we would persevere.

Our next greatest need came when we were ready to start selling the successful model we've built. We were profitable and into our new building but the personnel and HR systems and technology were not per par as we grew past 45 staff members. HR filing systems were likely out of compliance and not efficiently systemized and our technology was all outsourced. We were not advanced in these areas until I added an HR Director Emily M., Integration Manager Garrett E. and IT

Director Nader S. Our entire system went from amateur status to going full on pro status. These three vital positions have built the key elements we have now grown to be able to operate effectively and profitably with our sized system today. Our Executive Team is surround by passionate leaders and team members therefore the sky is limit with a mission that is as intense as ours.

This may sound robotic, but our people love their careers with Rejuv. Three years ago, I took the position of CEO of both companies as our team has doubled in size. I have had to come out of most the day to day to ensure the growth of both organizations. I have the main responsibility of ensuring success for our entire organization and helping the executives be successful in their roles. I am grateful for each person as none of this is possible without their buy-in and daily living of our core values.

The systems, policies, procedures and employees should be empowered to grow with your vision.

Where You Will Find The "Implementer":
Finding qualified employees is not a difficult thing to do, but the Fitness Director's position needs the most attention and will need to be the right fit for you. My experience was a great fit that

led to the Fitness Director position. I worked at Gold's Gym while I was in graduate school, so I also knew the best trainers they had when I started building Dr. Baumgartner's medical fitness practice. In my first year at Gold's, I was a sales representative and my first year after finishing my Bachelor's Degree I was a financial representative. Water towers and sports taught me team work and hard work is the key to lifelong success. Having two years' experience in a pure sales role was a critical steppingstone in selling our vision and transformation outcomes to prospects. Then while working in sales I found a love for nutrition and working out and I wanted to be a personal trainer. I studied everything I could to become the most effective trainer I could be. My passion for nutrition was a must for leading clients to transform their bodies.

I was also a patient of Dr. Baumgartner's, so essentially he had multiple interviews with me before I was ever offered the position. He knew I was the right candidate to build his medical fitness platform. Dr. Baumgartner later told me that in speaking with him he understood my passion for helping others and knew of the work ethic and drive I had. For the Implementer, you must take your time and make the right decision. From that point on, every employee you hire needs to share the same vision, values and know exactly what you're looking for, and be ready to do what it takes to make your vision a reality.

The first thing you want to do today is put an ad on Facebook, Linked In, Craigslist, or any agencies around the area describing the qualifications and position requirements. Communicating a well thought job description will be imperative to capture the right candidates and have a streamlined recruitment process. Due to my affiliation with the Medical Fitness Network, Medical Fitness Association, Functional Aging Institute, and our recruiting platform we post for all our partner facilities. I also conduct the interviews to see that we have the right skills that will increase the odds of having the right fit. I would also check local gyms for sales managers, or highly regarded personal trainers seeking a different career path. One of the most important qualifications, other than living a healthy lifestyle, is that they have the ability to do sales. You may find an extremely knowledgeable exercise physiologist, dietician, or trainer, but if they lack any sales experience they will struggle to grow your business. They may make a good team member or make good managers of your systems, but they need to have the ability to lead prospects to action. Too many medical professionals will try to sell with information instead of emotional hot buttons and the transformation possibilities. You can teach sales, so if you have the right person with the "it factor" it is still a possibility that they may be the right long-term successful fit. I will be able to train them, but I will need to see the numbers in our spreadsheet and have their full cooperation in order to close more than 80 percent of the prospects that come to your facility.

You want to find as many qualified candidates as possible to have group or phone interviews with. From there you will give the vision of the company and what you plan to achieve. Explain all of the systems and expectations of the position that you plan for them to follow. In this position, you do not want someone who wants to create a program the way they see it, but the way that your design is to be followed. Some people don't interview well, so only the final 10 or so will get one-on-one interviews; I would do this in a panel with your other team members. From there I would narrow it down to 3-4 for one-on-one interviews with you. Then you would want to narrow it down to two and go out to dinner with both and give them situations that will challenge them not to give canned answers, saying what they think you want to hear.

Once the Implementer is in place and you know they will be a great fit, it's time to expand your staff and let the director continue to make most of the decisions from here on out. The Implementer will report their scorecard to you on a weekly basis, but you will now be hands-off seeing masses of patients. Now it will be the Implementers role to put the next pieces of the puzzle together. I always recommend that once a new person is hired; you sit down with them to share your vision and the importance of each member's role. When people know why you do what you do, they will go to battle for you.

We also found that local colleges are a great location to find high quality and eager-to-learn MFS. You're not looking for someone who is great, but thinks they know it all because they won't follow your system. That just sets you up for a mess. With staff you hire, you or management should have a 90 day-introductory period while meeting each month to see if he or she will be a great fit and is meeting expectations to develop and fill in the gaps. As our facility continued to grow, we discovered that long-term patients who love everything about your program can also make great employees. We're definitely not looking for the everyday MFS. They need to live the part, be high-energy, great motivators, compassionate, caring, and want to change other people's lives while truly exemplifying our core values. You will know within that 3-month time frame if the candidate will be a long-term employee of your organization. As you grow I believe it's important to have one or two MFS with higher levels of experience, such as a Master's Degree in exercise physiology, to work with patients who are high-risk and who have injuries. Those who do not have a ton of experience can be taught if they have the skill-sets you seek. Each of our MFS need to be certified with one of the better recognized certifications to start with us.

From there we give them time to take our own medical certification process we have created.

How Much Will You Pay Your Medical Fitness Staff:

When hiring your Implementer and any other employees, you don't need to go out and spend thousands of dollars to hire a team to create something from scratch. Hand select those that match your core values, who are excited for this amazing vision and those motivated to be incentivized to help grow something special. We have found it is good to pay a fair market base and incentivize team members for your growth and success. Recognizing your employees holds much greater value than a high salary when starting as wages come as the biggest expense to a startup. If incentives are attached for positions each of your employees will be motivated to help the company grow in the right direction. Always have team meetings to communicate, as communication is proven to increase team morale and set goals to accomplish tasks that will continue to bring the practice forward. In addition to paying for continuing education, have other experts come in and speak to your staff educating them to be the best they can be. It's the same thing you would be telling them, but hearing it from another perspective can make another influential impact. Take your employees out to lunch and have staff gathering. Seek to be the inspiration and admirable company everyone wants to be a part of.

With the Implementer, you want to give out a base salary with incentives to grow. Percentage of the monthly net profit or EFT (Electronic Funds Transfer) and a profit-sharing model is the best method to motivate the Implementer to succeed. We also give a base salary to the assistant manager as well as commission from monthly sales. Your administrator will be paid straight hourly with multiple incentives for various services performed. Your MFS will be paid a percentage of each session trained, an hourly for specific job requirements such as team meetings, and incentives for various services and performance levels achieved.

On the clinical side of the practice, we work a production model of incentives as well as rewarding employees for outstanding service and in reaching a certain level of production. It is proven that practices and fitness facilities that operate with production-based models almost always outperform flat salaried practices. We offer a percentage of net collections, minus expenses that has bonus allotments as certain metrics are met for our providers.

Here is an example of a typical pay structure for non-salaried Medical Fitness Specialists:

Trainer Scale and Client Distribution:

White Level MFS
90-day Introductory Period.

MFS receives a 33% per session pay scale or $15 hourly rate depending on how you decide to pay. Hourly is recommended but each market must consider normal pay structures for MFS in your area.

$10/hour for all mandatory meetings & networking events, continuing education or required time.

Will receive clients after all advanced level MFS consideration was given first opportunity but any self-generated referral or lead goes directly to MFS responsible for bringing in patient.

Can advance when:

Client passes 90-day Introductory Period and has formal evaluation of continued employment.

Has brought in 2 referrals.

Follows all system checklists.

Successfully passes medical fitness certification.

Yellow Level MFS

MFS receives a 35% per session pay scale or $18 an hour.

$11/hour for all mandatory meetings, networking events, continuing education, sales opportunities or required time.

Will receive patients after Red Level MFS were given first consideration.

Can advance when:

Completed checklist documented in all files, following all systems.

Has a client retention percentage above 65%.

Has brought in 5 referrals.

Has 2 patient testimonials.

Maintaining over 25 hours of scheduled patients.

Red Level MFS

MFS receives a 37.5% per session pay scale or $20 hr.

$12/hour for all mandatory meetings and networking events, continuing education, sales opportunities or required time, and receives first opportunity on all new patients.

5% commission on any referral sales.

Can advance when:
Completed checklist documented in all files.
Following all systems.
Has a client retention percentage above 68%
Has brought in 10 referrals.
Has 5 patient testimonials.
30 hours of scheduled patients or classes to obtain full-time status with benefits at Blue Level. Must maintain full-time status for continued benefits.

Blue Level MFS
MFS receives a 40% per session pay scale and benefits if desired and maintains <u>full-time</u> status or $24/hour.
$13.50/hour for all mandatory meetings and networking events, continuing education, sales opportunities or required time, and receives first opportunity on all new patients after Black Level has no availability.
5% commission on any referral sales.

Can advance when:
Has a client retention percentage above 72%.
Has brought in 20 referrals.
Has 10 patient testimonials.
Maintaining over 32 hours of scheduled patients or classes.

Black Level MFS
MFS receives a 42% per session pay scale and benefits or $28 hr.
$15/hour for all mandatory meetings and networking events, continuing education, sales opportunities or required time, and receives first opportunity on all new clients.
5% commission on any referral sales and 5% of maintained EFT for their patients.

Chapter 5

The Six Step Medical Fitness I.M.P.A.C.T. Plan

<u>Automation and Core Processes Create Freedom & Scalability</u>

An essential element to fully comprehend is for your organization to scale and grow you must break down each core process so that your entire organization understands how to operate. Automation and systems are the only way to be efficient, avoid waste, have consistency with employee and patient relations, outcomes with patients, reduce costs and grow without major pain. We grew very fast and we lacked any formal systems, core processes and we nearly lost everything and had to stop growing for a period of time and start building our foundation from scratch. We had to develop core process for our major business functions. We did not create a 200-page manual rather capturing the important steps of each major functions in a 30-page document that gives an overview of our entire operating system. We used The Parettos' Principal, that 20% of the most important details will provide 80% of the information our team and patients need to know about our process. Each department head such as our accountant may have many more steps and details for our Financial Core Process they navigate through however, our MFS don't need to know that, they just need to know about payment polices, reimbursement, payroll, benefits, etc.

Once you establish core processes you can begin to create systems that automate the steps of the workflow. Below I have outlined a brief description of each process. The purpose of this book is to keep as short and sweet as possible as a review to the necessary components for a successful medical fitness practice. The what is for you to implement as your practice has different products services and would require its own special design.

Marketing Core Process:
The process of obtaining leads in today's market is through consistent content and relationship management. How you maximize the different platforms is how well you manage your time and use technical applications. It is essential to leverage your content in as many mediums possible in the timeliest manner to create omnipresence.

The more leads you get, especially when you get better at marketing, won't be ready to join your programs right away. They need a little more convincing.

Keys to nurturing your leads forward:

- Construct a prospect workflow to follow up via text, phone, email and social media.
- Generate an email autoresponder to share valuable content with your leads.
- Provide opportunities approximately once per month to join your front-end offer or other special promotional programs on landing pages.
- Establish opportunities like workshops and seminars to get them in your facility and in front of you.

There are certain media applications, such as Tweet Deck, that allow you to take one post to post to all of your social sites and it's easy to pull off.

Monitoring your results is also a part of the process. This is critical for split testing ads, dropping what does not convert and maximizing what is working. Having a team that understands the flow of lead acquisition, follow up and tracking is essential to go from good to great.

Sales Process:

A consistent and scalable sales process, I may be a little biased, is the most important of all business functions for profitability, scaling and growing. It's almost a toss-up between that and getting results with patients but you must get them started to get results.

Without being great on this end I find it very difficult for a cash based practice or business to succeed in the competitive health, fitness and cash medicine industry. I could write a book on helping people buy your services as there are thousands of books and styles on how to be a successful sales professional. I do not sell, I coach. In order to effectively block out the selling fear employees may face; this is what we teach our team. We prefer the term "assistant buyer" or "trusted advisor," and use push-away sales as opposed to hard selling. As a medical facility, we do not want the reputation of pushing people into products and services they don't want or are ready to commit to. Our dedicated sales staff are called Patient Advocates or Regenerative Communication Specialists, not sales professionals. It's the subtle assignment of aiding our prospects achieve their desired outcomes.

People are turned off by gyms, facilities and professionals that push people into decisions they are uncomfortable with. There is a fine art to recommending and selling services. Our licensees will go through our intense sales training program to help more people make the best decision for themselves by asking important and reflective questions and really not selling at all.

The skills we teach have allowed our Fitness Director and Patient Advocates to sell over $1,200,000 in our facility in each of the last two years.

This chapter is not based on theories. We have been trained by the most successful industry leaders and have combined all the best practices and applied them to medical fitness. The goal of this book, and more specifically the sales process, is to assist you in attracting, selling, and retaining high paying and compliant patients because you provide the best service value and results. I want you to try and embrace the beauty of helping others instead of thinking of it as sales. From an operating standpoint, new sales are the most critical factor for the success of your medical fitness facility. Yes, of course you must bring an amazing experience and deliver results.

The whole sales process is dictated by the mindset one has regarding the situation. Employees, and people in general, see sales as making people do something they don't want or that they themselves wouldn't personally need to invest in. For instance, a personal trainer may have a hard time selling a $380 a month program when they could not afford that themselves or because they already live a healthy lifestyle and wouldn't need the professional help. When they project their thoughts to prospects it is hard for them to inspire people to begin the journey. The funny thing is it's the exact opposite. It's about helping people get what they want and then assisting them in the process. Everyone we speak to wants to lose weight or change their body or lifestyle or overall health. People see sales as taking advantage of people rather than giving them the tools to be successful. They see it as talking people into why their product or service is the best and not listening to what the prospect wants. They hear the sales term "close," but I see it as opening people up for change, and joy and happiness that they may have been lacking. Those that cannot sell see it as forcing someone to do something. I only see it as "What can I give these people?" I love the slogan the Biggest Loser uses: "Pay It Forward." We can make a difference. We are not in "the business of selling," it is "the practice of changing and giving people what they want." Selling is helping the prospect to value the benefits of your services the way you see them. It's transference of feelings from you to another. Your responsibility is helping the prospect believe the benefits of living the same lifestyle that you do. The prospect will live longer, healthier, and with more complete joy if you show them that value and share the hope that your services can be a solution to their desired transformation.

The one thing we ask our employees to remember is that this person is going to have a healthier life in some fashion because of the experience we provide. If you have that focus and you truly believe that your service will benefit someone, it's your obligation to motivate and challenge that person to change and make the investment in themselves. The best sales staff and employees are not those who are great closers or slimy sales professionals. They are great because of the goodwill and passion they get out of helping others. It drives them to make people healthier and to live better lives. Your job as the assistant buyer or trusted advisor is to help that person trust you to guide them to the solutions they seek.

You must explain to your sales staff, MFS, and providers that you are not a sales person; you are a life changer. You are not an order-taker, you are a prescriber. My weight loss sales staff will not let a person who has a good amount of weight to lose say, "I just want to buy four sessions." We prescribe a program that is going to set someone up to succeed. We don't allow patients to dictate the way we provide treatment, otherwise we would not be doctors or professionals. The same thing goes for weight loss. The prospect would not be sitting in front of you if they didn't need the education, accountability, support, inspiration or motivation to get long-lasting results.

If your staff doesn't live by the prescription policy, you will not get people started in your programs, and you will not give them the results they need to be successful long term. For this reason alone, you must follow a proven and predictable conversion system. If you don't, you will fail to help as many people as possible and your practice will struggle no matter how many marketing leads you get. Thus, all your marketing dollars will be for nothing. I had one group that was getting over 20 leads a week but was closing only around one. I had to inform the group that we had to replace this person as there was no hope with these types of numbers despite his care and passion to help others.

It's easy to train your staff in the sales process. It's not difficult to learn how to build relationships, how to focus on prospects' needs and wants, how to communicate your unique program for transformation, how to understand each person's emotional hot buttons, how to handle objections before they even occur, and how to invite the prospect into transformation. Each employee should know the basics. It's your direct sales staff that is meeting with new prospects that needs to be well rehearsed to assist people in beginning their journey. Time needs to be dedicated to finding the person who can build relationships by being caring, sympathetic, trustworthy, judgment free, and a great coach. They need to bring hope, energy, and enthusiasm to every appointment. I call it the "IT" factor. Some have it, some don't. Although the traits I mentioned are great, it's not critical if they are lacking a boisterous personality. All they must do is follow the systems provided and be able to listen to clients' needs and wants.

Sales staff and employees who listen and learn the subtle words the prospects will provide, will be the most successful. Find the person who can open the prospect up and not close them down, and you will have new patients. Books like the *Go Giver* and *Low Profile Seller* help give a fundamental understanding of how, through sales, you can help more people and at the same time feel positive about the difference you are making in people's lives when you get them on the right program.

Financial Core Process:

Accountant:
- Review bank account balances and credit card balances daily
- Reconcile bank account balances and credit card balances monthly
- Using various reports received from various departments, prepare cash basis financial statements for JR's review
- Process payroll biweekly
- Process quarterly and annual sales tax & provider tax returns
- Prepare items for annual tax return & year end payroll
- Member of MindBody task force reconcile all numbers and tie out correctly
- Verify that intercompany accounts reconcile

Front Office:

- Greet and check in guests – demographics – insurance intake
- Collect balances on accounts and co-pays
- PCC's count out tills at end of day
- Prepare deposit slip
- Take deposits to bank

Back Office:

- All of the front office duties plus the following:
- Daily Close out reports
- Calculate trainers, esthetics and massage therapists' biweekly payroll
- Track trade agreements
- Member of MindBody task force
- Keeps petty cash

Billing:

- Process monthly billing
- Receive Payments
- Make deposit in Mind Body
- Collections/Payment Plans

Accounting Asst:

- Receive invoices that have been approved for payment
- Enter invoices into QuickBooks for payment
- Pay bills by cutting checks weekly
- Attach check to invoice being paid and bring checks to JR for signature
- Mail out signed checks
- Reconcile petty cash
- Cut checks for approved reimbursements

Gym Core Process:

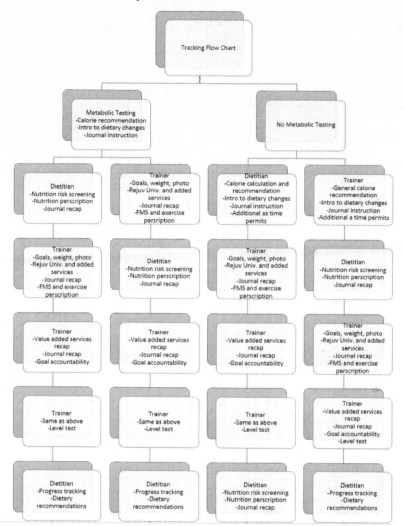

Tracking Flow Chart

Metabolic Testing
-Calorie recommendation
-Intro to dietary changes
-Journal instruction

No Metabolic Testing

Dietitian -Nutrition risk screening -Nutrition perscription -Journal recap	**Trainer** -Goals, weight, photo -Rejuv Univ. and added services -Journal recap -FMS and exercise persription	**Dietitian** -Calorie calculation and recommendation -Intro to dietary changes -Journal instruction -Additional as time permits	**Trainer** -General calorie recommendation -Intro to dietary changes -Journal instruction -Additional a time permits
Trainer -Goals, weight, photo -Rejuv Univ. and added services -Journal recap -FMS and exercise perscription	**Dietitian** -Nutrition risk screening -Nutrition perscription -Journal recap	**Trainer** -Goals, weight, photo -Rejuv Univ. and added services -Journal recap -FMS and exercise perscription	**Dietitian** -Nutrition risk screening -Nutrition perscription -Journal recap
Trainer -Value added services recap -Journal recap -Goal accountability	**Trainer** -Value added services recap -Journal recap -Goal accountability	**Trainer** -Value added services recap -Journal recap -Goal accountability	**Trainer** -Goals, weight, photo -Rejuv Univ. and added services -Journal recap -FMS and exercise perscription
Trainer -Same as above -Level test	**Trainer** -Same as above -Level test	**Trainer** -Same as above -Level test	**Trainer** -Value added services recap -Journal recap -Goal accountability -Level test
Dietitian -Progress tracking -Dietary recommendations	**Dietitian** -Progress tracking -Dietary recommendations	**Dietitian** -Nutrition risk screening -Nutrition perscription -Journal recap	**Dietitian** -Progress tracking -Dietary recommendations

There are many a few routes patients can go depending on if they integrate medically either by cash or insurance. The above graphic is if they choose any cash based medical services or go directly into training. Our goal is to get them started as soon as possible and depending on scheduling order and availability the patient may see someone different for their first session. Each new patient's information will be filed in the MFS's binder to make sure all core aspects of the fitness program are covered by the MFS. We have different client tracking software and a plateau training module to track results and offer coaching and alternative solutions to any roadblocks to reaching goals. The most important factor is that you have a process that is understood, effective and followed by all.

Clinic Patient Flow Core Process:

Explaining how we diligently focused to automate our clinic patient flow to save thousands of hours a year is beneficial to share. We used to have a new patient packet that we had them fill out when they arrived. We quickly found many patients showed up not 30 min before their appointment like we requested to complete the necessary paperwork, setting the entire schedule behind. As a first step, we started e-mailing patients the packet at the time of scheduling and communicated to be there 30 minutes prior to appointment if not filled out, and 15 minutes if already complete. That helped some but several times a day patients still had incomplete packets. A next phase was during the reminder calls to explain the same, and even a little better. A new EHR allowed us to do follow up reminders with text and e-mail and phone call. The last step was if the new patient the packet must be entered through the online appointment unless they do not have access to a computer. This in turn then populates into the record and saves an assistant the first 15 minutes of every new patient when this is done. This is just one simple example of how we need to look at each system and see if there are ways to improve efficiencies. We utilize a process called Lean and Traction to continue to revisit each initiative for new ideas and technological enhancements that save time and money. Each improvement allows us to benefit more patients and keep cost of care stable as we grow.

Human Resources Core Process:

Below is a brief outline of a top-level example of posting for a new position thru employment termination. This is for our staff to see but the HR Director has several components and documents that work into this flow that have proven effective.

Intake Need
    Assess overall needs
    Define role/create job description
    Wage assessment

Recruitment
>Post position website/social media/schools/networking sites/Career Plug

Interview
>Pre-Screen/Phone Call
>>Or Decline
>
>Interview
>>1st round formal in-person
>>2nd round formal in-person/shadow opportunity
>>Or Decline

Background Check/Kolbe Test

Hiring/Extend Offers
>Letter/Benefits/Dress code/Job Description

Orientation
>First Day Orientation
>Notification to appropriate team members/all company communication
>Specific job training orientation/shadowing
>30/60/90 Introductory Visits – Goal setting
>Annual/Anniversary Date – Ongoing merit and goal setting opportunities
>Compliance Module

Performance Improvement Plan – PIP
>As needed

Ongoing Benefits Management
>Health
>401(k)
>FMLA
>Work Comp
>EAP
>Supplemental
>LOA

Warning Systems
    Verbal/Written
    As needed

Termination
    Letter/Benefits Handout
    Exit interview
    Notification to appropriate team members/all company communication
    Compliance Checklist Completed

The truth of core processes is simple. If it's not documented there will come a point in time where it needs to be if ever expected to be understood and practiced by all.

Chapter 6

The Six Step Medical Fitness I.M.P.A.C.T. Plan
(C.): Communication for Clinical Success

The business life of your practice is predicated via your ability to communicate to your target market and amongst your team. With patients, they must have a desire for something you provide and you can fill that void. In turn, their life will be better because of your relationship. At the same time, you must deliver your service in a caring way that shows you are doing everything to protect them. As you grow beyond more than one team member things can easily be miscommunicated and misconstrued if you do not harness the need for clear communication as a major focus of your organization.

Communicating effectively is and will always be a committed focus as an essential key component to our success. We have had many communication gaps in the past that have needed to be addressed time and time again. Core process, operational systems, employment process all need to be consistently adhered to throughout the organization. For that to be a reality the team must understand why each function of our system is necessary.

The only way we were going to adapt and grow is advancing all of our communication channels. For an overview, it's too difficult to dive into our communication systems and use of technology as it is broad and intensely vital to capture each in and out. For this overview, specifically 'how' we communicate is more important. We have used Traction EOS to improve communications throughout our organization. This is a management/leadership entrepreneurial operating system that involves the entire organization. In short, it's a communication and delivery method involving everyone into the business of the mission at hand. From the mission, vision, core values, core processes, business plan, meetings structures, communication platforms, metrics reporting, separated by department, weekly, monthly, yearly and beyond goals for your organization. We are only two years into the process and have made serious strides at fostering interdepartmental communication and cooperation with the use of this system. The Executive Team commits to weekly, quarterly, and annual communication meetings. Every other department meets weekly as needed and directors communicate to the Executive Team so we all work together to execute the quarterly and yearly goals(rocks).

Below is a diagram of our basic Traction vision.

CORE VALUES	1. **Virtuous** – We check our egos at the door, we are humble and loyal to each other as we listen and create a unified synergy with patients and our team. 2. **Brilliant** – We are unique pioneers. We are growth-minded and strive for excellence. 3. **Results** – We are here to change healthcare by restoring health and vitality in our patients. Our outcome-based approach will hold us accountable. Quality care with quality outcomes	**3-YEAR PICTURE"** Future Date: 12/31/2018 Revenue: $11,000,000 Waite Park ($3,000,000 MedFit) Profit: (30% Net Profit)
CORE FOCUS"	Purpose: Restoring health worldwide Our Niche: Through integrating regenerative orthopedics, functional medicine, and medical fitness.	Measurables: What does it look like? • 100-120 Employees • 7 FT Physicians, 4 FT Nurse Practitioners, 2 Physician Assis • Extended Hours • 1,700 Gym Members & 360 CrossFit Members
5-YEAR TARGET"	350 Locations (Communities Impacted) Worldwide through the sales of Licenses, Masterminds, and Franchises. As of 6/14/2016 count of 31.	• MedDoors producing $400,000 revenue • 1,500,000 in Corporate Wellness Accounts • Build out of the building to include business offices and gym • Formulate Corporate Partnerships – MRI's, Surgeons, etc.
MARKETING STRATEGY	Target Market/"The List": 30-50 yr old motivated and informed health conscious patient who suffers from chronic degeneration or fitness related issues Three Uniques: 1. Regenerative Orthopedics 2. Functional Medicine 3. Medical Fitness 4. Integrated outcome driven Proven Process: C-FAN (Cell Health, Functional Movement, Articulation, Nerve Health) Guarantee: A comprehensive approach to partner with patients to maximize their outcomes	• Develop efficiencies to better utilize technology • Patented App-Based System fully operational • CFO Role • Online-training module • Have all insurance contracts (any willing provider act)

Can you articulate exactly how to achieve the desired outcome patients seek? Your patient has no idea what that looks like or how to achieve that result, nor do they have the confidence. It's you and your staff's understanding of this that makes you the best. Per Jay Abraham, author of *Getting Everything You Can Out of All You Got*, every one of the staff members working with your patients will need to share your same core mission by using the Strategy of Preeminence:

1) **Empathy** - A true passion to help your patients change their lives.
2) **Leadership** - Taking authoritative charge for their health by being a leader. It's your confidence, knowledge, and direction that will lead them to long-term change. You will be their trusted advisor for life. You will always be there. You are their hero.

3) **Understanding** - "I know how you must feel." You must relate to their fears, dreams, and goals. The more they feel you know them, the more they will sing praise. The more personal touch you can provide, the better.

4) **Focus** – Provides patients with clarity and certainty. Clean-cut directions to attain their goal, and how you can help them one step at a time. The ability to give them the life they want through your focus and guidance. You are committed to them as their leader; that your path is different and unique and you will guide them there with a relationship!

5) **Connectivity** - You will connect all of the dots for them, and you know better than anyone what they need.

Jay States, "Being preeminent is the foundation of everything you are and do." We use phrases like this all the time. "I will not let you continue to let your body down." "This is what you need." "I will not let you not achieve your goal." With medical knowledge, you understand what an unhealthy lifestyle does to a person. You have a responsibility to help them change. You have a responsibility to make their life better mentally, physically, and spiritually. You are responsible to them, but not for them. With the right guidance, we have the opportunity change lives. Providing extreme value to your patients is the biggest and most powerful factor for guaranteeing a long business life for your practice. Patients must feel welcomed, respected, loved and protected.

One of our trainers continued to struggle to get results for patients and retain them for longer than a month or two at a time. She continued to tell me, "It's not my fault that they won't listen." I said, "You're right, it may not be your fault, but it is your responsibility to help lead them to their goal." The entire team is vigilant to the development of patient-centered care skills and any practitioner or coach on their coaching skills so we can help guide patients to greater success.

15 Tips for you and your staff to live by:

1) In speaking with patients, you must be politely transparent
2) Don't let them feel out of control
3) People need solutions that they agree to, not just strategies
4) Don't bedazzle them with how great you are
5) Be great and make sense, respect their intelligence, change their lives
6) Always show them where they were and how they are heading towards their goal
7) Show them how far they have come and how important every small change is
8) Give patients ways to validate their decisions
9) Always be hopeful
10) Show them you understand and listen to their needs
11) Coach, people get lost in information; they seek a solution that works for them
12) Without trust, they will not act, they won't change who they are
13) Always use ways of communicating and systematic follow up a priority
14) Live in the positive, greet people with excitement
15) Always be thinking: How many more lives will I improve and help today?

I have found the greater a personal can develop at communicating with patients and giving them what they want and need, the better success will be obtained in all walks of life. Effective communication is one of the best skills to develop and obtain. I have grown as I've become an experienced communicator however I still must develop this skill even further to expand our mission the next level of intensity.

Chapter 7

The Six Step Medical Fitness I.M.P.A.C.T. Plan

(T.) Training and Corporate Wellness Programs for Any Practice

When deciding which model to incorporate, there are several considerations one must first navigate. First, have a plan of what business goals your medical fitness program will serve. Will your fitness program be a funnel for your medical practice, used to get your current patients greater outcomes or are you looking to maximize revenue opportunities? Are you going to be working with only high-risk populations and the elderly? Are you in a location that will have enough square footage to provide you the opportunity to run group sessions? All of these questions need to be considered before diving into a medical fitness business venture.

Our program started out in a room the size of many people's home closets. There was no way we could have run group classes. One-on-one training was the only option. When I reached a full schedule, I hired two trainers and we could use a Snap Fitness facility as long as we paid monthly memberships for each client. When summer came around we started running fitness boot camps outdoors. We also started working with local high school teams by going to their school and running workouts in their weight room and on the football field. Once we had enough clients, we knew we would need a much larger space, so we began our search for a standalone workout facility large enough to fit our needs. The one downfall of this facility was that it would have to be separate from our medical clinic.

Once we had enough space, we could operate any type of fitness programs without limitations. If you have the generous size, it will be an option to run different types of fitness programs. These different fitness programs include: one-on-one, semi-private, boot camps, medically supervised training, and athletic and corporate wellness programs. Each of the programs have their need in the market and will each be explained further. This book will discuss the model and principles of each type of fitness programs that are available, but not to demonstrate the programming of each one. Our licensees will be given extensive training on the assessment, programming, and implementation of all topics related to your training programs.

Medically Supervised Training:

Any programs that are supervised or delivered by medical professionals as an extension of a medical provider are called medically supervised training programs. These programs are usually billed through insurance as licensed medical staff will administer or supervise the programs. Medically supervised training is the most common program with a patient who has diagnosis codes, which would allow you to bill through insurance. There are a few current models for this type of programming. If the diagnosis codes allow you to bill, you may have the option to have an exercise physiologist/physical therapy assistant administer the workouts that were designed by an MD or physical therapist. In this instance, it is much easier to bill through insurance with a diagnosis of physical injury as opposed to an obesity diagnosis. However, certain insurance companies are allocating a specific number of dollars to be given to any patients who have an obesity diagnosis.

Medically supervised programs will have a higher profit margin than cash-based personal training services due to insurance reimbursements. The barrier to entry is easiest for the patient as they are not paying cash out of their pockets if insurance will cover medically supervised training. Even though the program is processed through insurance, each patient would still be responsible for their insurance deductible. We have found that in most cases those who may be classified as high-risk or have one or more physical limitations, usually will reach their deductible one way or another and this is not a barrier to entry.

A major consideration is that the United States Supreme Court upheld the Affordable Care Act. Our healthcare system is in desperate need of solutions due to the rising cost of healthcare and increasing incidents of metabolic-related disease due to obesity. The need for medically supervised fitness-based programs that teach proper nutrition and exercise has never been more desperately needed until now. I can almost guarantee that in the next two to four years there will be thousands of programs similar to what we have created. There are strong movements in the medical fitness arena that are advocating for insurance-based coverage for facilities such as ours. Clinics that are medically fitness integrated will help fill the void between long-term prevention and treatment.

One-On-One Training:

This is the model that has catapulted our success in the shortest amount of time. Although it is not directly supervised by medical professionals, we rely highly on our medical clinic to better provide solutions for our patients. We can offer physicals, metabolic testing, food allergy and sensitivity testing, bio-identical hormone balancing, functional medicine labs and injury treatment and therapy. A large portion of the population is interested in losing weight or learning to live a healthier lifestyle. When they come in for a consultation they are asking to lose weight or learn to exercise and eat better. The medical testing can help identify the best methods for doing so or get them past a plateau. The only difference is that we are using personal trainers to deliver the exercise and nutrition guidelines. Don't get me wrong, if they need to see our dietician or our physical therapist, we recommend they do so. We just communicate back to our medical fitness specialists the limitations or recommendations of our medical findings.

People come to us because we are different than a gym. When you have the medical name, it is much more trusted than a standalone gym. When we have clear direction from medical staff, we are better able to serve those who have any complications or have any health considerations. We have an extensive certification program for our MFS's that prepare them to help those with various medical-related conditions and injuries. It is a great synergistic effect that our patients receive when working with us towards a common goal.

We highly recommend that anyone who is starting a program to begin with our one-on-one training programs. Once we are confident that the patients have proper exercise form and understand what healthy nutrition is, we are happy to advance them to group training or boot camps.

As far as profits are concerned, a one-on-one training studio alone is not a large source for profits. Once in our standalone we had over 180 clients and we were still not sure why we were not profiting as initially. The reason is when you perform one-on-one training the net profits are meager after paying the cost of your trainer and the expenses of running your practice. Now don't get me wrong, you will still see a huge increase of revenue in your medical practice due to the one-on-one training that you refer to the clinic for lab testing, office visits, etc., but if you do the accounting as two separate entities as we have, the margins for one-on-one training are small compared to reimbursable programs, group training, or boot camps. However, it's about the broader picture of being able to help so many people and having a massive funnel to your medical clinic with even more potential for higher reimbursements and enhanced patient outcomes.

Group Training:

By far one of the most effective ways of training today is group personal training. This means anywhere from 2- 8 people with similar goals, conditioning, and experience at one time. As a medically integrated fitness studio, you can help more people at one time using this model. They all have the same access to your medical services and program offerings although they are just training in a group as opposed to one-on-one.

With small group training, you can earn hundreds of dollars per hour. When training three, six, or eight clients at one time, the practice will make far more money for your time than with the one-on-one model. Using the semi-private training model, Medical Fitness Specialists (MFS) can work part-time hours while making as much as a full-time MFS. We want to make sure we can retain high quality staff so full-time MFS have the ability to make a more fruitful living than working at a typical gym. We charge $35 per person for an hour-long session. If training one-on-one, an hour workout would be around $80. In addition, it is more affordable for your patients and the profit margin is much higher for your facility. If you have five people it becomes a $175-hour session. If you can fill up your busy hours with semi-private sessions, you will see your net profits rise dramatically. If you have only one-on-one sessions, you will have several starving MFS as they will all be full during the hours between 4-7pm. When they get full, you will need to hire another MFS. It is very important that you begin to develop semi-private training once you are established.

With group training your workouts are almost always fun, exciting, and fast paced so patients love the workouts. When you have this system in place you will also obtain more referrals, because you have access to more clients. Once you establish this type of environment and culture, if you lose a patient it is easy to find another person to add into the group. The greatest benefit is that you will help more patients in less time. With group personal training, because you combine the individual attention and progression of personal training with the high energy of boot camps, you're able to get more people into shape than with other forms of training. Small groups are much easier to manage than huge boot camps and the risk of injury is far less when you can monitor form.

With small group personal training, you will acquire the intense camaraderie, competitiveness, and high energy of a boot camp while still being able to keep everyone's form spot on and make sure they progress in each exercise like with private personal training. It truly is combining the best of both worlds for the ideal training experience for you and your patients.

Another major consideration is the lifetime value per client with group personal training. You have a much higher average retention rate than with one-on-one training because the workouts are far more affordable and you're able to charge prices that your average client can afford for a long period of time. Group training also builds a support system clients will need to stay active and healthy on their journey. You will immediately find the group is committed and accountable. When one person misses a session, we make everyone in the group do "get well" burpees or pushups, and have everyone in the group text the missing person. You can't get that type of accountability with one-on-one. For the patients, they don't want to miss out on spending time with like-minded friends all seeking to enrich their lives.

Boot Camps:

Boot Camps are a growing industry and a great way to get a lot of people in shape and provide challenging workouts. Boot camp exercise classes vary in style, depending on the teacher. But you can generally expect to be challenged on all aspects of working out. It's an hour or half-hour doing some form of cardiovascular exercise such as running, hiking, interval training, or obstacle course challenges, and strength elements using dumbbells, exercise bands, the resistance of your own body weight and every other piece of fitness equipment you can dream up. We also focus on flexibility in a stretch portion of the class, which may incorporate yoga or Pilates elements. We have beginner weight loss boot camps and advanced boot camps so we can cater to two different populations.

With boot camps, people can come as often as they like without having to book a set time. Boot camp classes are offered for defined periods of time. We have 30 set classes per week. By offering different times, people can come without an appointment and whenever it works into their personal schedule. This is usually easiest for clients, but it does have its disadvantages.

It can be difficult to progress your clients in a way you can with personal training. Another difficulty is sometimes you will have people who will want to come five days a week and that can be hard on the body if you are hitting the same muscle groups every day. The sessions are designed to give a great overall workout and are not specifically designed for one person.

You will have numbers ranging from 5- 30 people and you must design your workouts to keep people moving at all times. The drawback is when you have the high attendance numbers it is difficult to keep a close eye on form. The risk of injury is higher in a boot camp setting as compared to a one-on-one workout. Therefore, we prefer all of our patients to start with personal training or semi-private group training before moving on to boot camps. By doing this, we can teach proper form and lay down the nutrition foundation so people can see results and minimize risk of injury.

The major benefits of a boot camp are that you can charge a set amount of money and have low overhead. We charge $127 a month and can provide impressive workouts and a high-energy patent experience for an affordable price. This can be much more affordable for the patient as compared to one-on-one, or semi-private group training. Much like group training, the earnings are much higher than a one-on-one session. This can provide your facility with the highest net return. In conclusion, we include each of these programs into our facility. It truly depends on where you are starting and your facility considerations. The more patients you have, the more options you will want to add. I know multiple people in the industry who only specialize in one or two of these options. It's all about finding out who you want to serve and the type of business structure you desire. For example, if you are only going to market to the high-risk or elderly population I would probably only focus on the medically supervised, personal, and semi-private training model. When appropriately rolled out and managed, they all can be very successful.

Online Training:

The wave of the future will come in forms of online training, health coaching, telemedicine usage through digital course work, group and individual webcasts. Our online platform has allowed us to reach far more communities worldwide and we have just begun the journey. Patients and prospects in our community and globally are looking for more affordable and time convenient care with no geographical boundaries. By not taking proactive steps to the future of medicine, this is a major oversight in my opinion. Most training, coaching and functional medicine can be performed digitally with ease once workable technical systems are put in place. These types of programs offer greater margins for the practice, more affordable and detailed care for patients, and significant time savings for medical and fitness service providers. Inside our licensing and coaching program, we are setting up online systems for practices to improve current margins and stay a step ahead of the next shift in healthcare.

Corporate Wellness:

Corporate opportunities lend a significant opportunity for medically supervised programs. Insurance costs continue to rise for employers. There are many options to help companies grow their wellness programs with costs that fit any companies budget. Everything discussed in the online training section of this chapter can be effectively delivered to companies. Healthy and motivated employees are critical to the workplace. Unhealthy employees can negatively affect the bottom line of corporations in expenditures on insurance and absenteeism, overall affecting revenue.

Much of your work force will spend more hours at work than anywhere else, in addition to the time they spend commuting each day. In fact, the typical American works approximately 47 hours a week, which is at least 164 more hours yearly than the average for 20 years ago. Given these statistics, it is easy to see why maintaining a healthy work/life balance is becoming increasingly essential. Corporate wellness programs are important tools to establish this balance. Programs that emphasize the benefits of corporate wellness can be implemented in a variety of styles.

One of the primary benefits of corporate wellness involves a reduction in the rates of illness and injuries among employees while globally reducing chronic disease and metabolic syndrome. Unhealthy employees experience a wide range of work-related injuries such as muscle strain, carpal tunnel syndrome, stress fractures, and/or back pain. High-risk individuals are also susceptible to developing complications such as diabetes, heart disease, and/or a stroke. Employees without the opportunity to participate in corporate wellness programs may develop serious illnesses. Consequently, they could find themselves on long-term disability for an extended period or be forced to discontinue working entirely.

In addition to preventing illnesses amongst employees, corporate wellness programs also lead to a reduction in employee absenteeism. Employees who are stressed, unhealthy, or overworked tend to become sick more often than healthy employees. When programs that focus on the benefits of corporate wellness are implemented, this rate can be drastically reduced. For example, Coors Brewing Company experienced a remarkable 18% decrease in employee absenteeism after implementing a corporate wellness program within their workplace.

Another benefit of corporate wellness programming is a reduction in the cost of health care. When employees are healthy and less stressed, they tend to rely less on costly programs such as disability insurance and sick leave. Over the last two years while the majority of companies have experienced 25-40% increases we have not had a single increase due to a healthy workforce. Our premiums have not increased; they have remained the same. Companies will notice a significant decrease in health care costs once they incorporate wellness programs into their workplace. For example, after implementing a fitness program in which only 60% of the employees participated, Coca-Cola could save $500 per employee every year.

Corporate wellness programs also contribute to the enhanced retention of key employees. Companies that implement wellness programs typically experience a much lower rate of employee turnover. Recruiting, marketing, and advertising for vacant positions are very costly, not to mention time-consuming. If your employees are happy and healthy and enjoy working at your company odds are they are more likely to be retained. Employees with health and fitness benefits have reported they feel that the companies care about them personally and this fosters a strong sense of community and commitment from the staff in the organization.

Increased productivity is another benefit of corporate wellness. Employees who are fulfilled and healthy tend to produce a greater volume of work at a higher quality than unhealthy employees. Employers need to realize that implementing health and fitness programs will lower stress levels and increase the overall output of their employees. Many executives and owners look only at the added costs versus the long-term investment and savings such programs have been proven to show.

Our goal is to lead companies to experience a reduction in employee injuries, illness, absenteeism and health care costs, as well as an increase in employee retention and productivity. Assuming responsibility for establishing a healthy, harmonious working environment, this will allow everyone to relish in the benefits of corporate wellness.

Chapter 8

The 12 Should Ask Questions Before Starting a Medical Fitness Practice

1) For the practices that experience success, what is the most important factor for growth besides the right people who can sell and launch the program off the ground?

I would say that the answer is the same for your fitness program as it is for your clinic. Building a sustainable and successful practice without proven outcomes and results is nearly impossible. Having the right staff and a solid marketing plan to get prospects into your funnel are the two leading factors for growing. Those alone are simply not enough. Even with terrible marketing, your business can grow slowly as long as you are superior to anything else that exists in your market place. You get referrals when you get results and this is our number one way we acquire new patients. Being acknowledged for results helps you stand out compared to any competition in the area. Providing extreme value and results to your patients is the biggest and most powerful factor for guaranteeing a long business life for your practice.

Patients must feel welcomed, respected, loved and protected. There must be systems in place that allow your patients to get the desired results they seek. After years of practice, for me personally it was easy for me to coach people to see results. Many of my subsequent hires did not have the same skills so I had to create systems and our organizations shifted to employee development training programs with the basis of how achieve, maximize and retain results.

When we meet with patients we must build rapport and be honest with the gaps they will need fill to attain results in a very compassionate and caring manner. When someone is morbidly obese and says they just want to go once a week for just a month, I know I am failing that client by not saying they need a year program three times a week. Someone who is inactive and is seeing a physical therapist will not get better once a week. We need to see them a minimum of three times a week.

Not offering up-sells and telling them the most effective, fastest, and proven methods of getting results is considered not caring enough for your patient. For example, if we sell a training package and stop right there, we have not provided the most effective way to get results. After you advise them into buying training, your next line should be, "By the way, here are three supplements that will help you see the best results," or "I know your knee hurts. I should have you meet with the doctor first." You must advise them on what will be best and not look at it as sales. You don't need their money; you truly desire them to reach their goals. It's being an assistant buyer and a trusted advisor, not a salesman.

It's okay if a patient chooses not to follow exactly what you recommend, but the point is you must offer them the best path to their goal. Once you have done that, you will continue to show your value to patients. It's not just about results; it's about impacting lives.

We focus most our staff training on how to retain patients and get the best results possible. We educate the reasons why paying clients stop training. The goal is to retain 72% of our fitness patients for a minimum of 6 months. This is the only way we can have a long-term impact. Below are the 3 categories clients fall under when they leave.

1) No results - They will not pay what we charge without results unless you are filling another need.
2) The value in the relationship has changed - Not the same trainer value, too comfortable, more like friends now, hit goal, more affordable elsewhere.
3) Poor experience - Customer service, unfriendliness, no connectivity, dirty.

2) What are the most important staffing lessons you have learned in any licensed programs that have failed?

We have failed in seven locations now. I can narrow it down to five reasons for the failures.

1) In four occasions the main Implementers were not paid what they believe was fair or were unhappy with the long-term growth plan. In two of the instances I believe that to be true and the others did not take an ethical route in my opinion. They took the patients and started their own business. I recommend a proper incentive based performance structure, profit sharing model and possible ownership options once proven. Just in case the first person cannot handle the Implementer role I believe it is very important getting in a second trainer as fast as possible so if they leave or can't handle the responsibility of growing the program you are not starting from scratch. I have had a handful trainers at our facility leave to start their own business and only two did it the right way. This is the nature of the training business at times. Amongst all of them only one is making more than they were as a trainer at our facility and he was the most skilled all around. He was my fitness director after I was promoted to CFO/Practice Administrator and he learned the skills

necessary to write his own story. Non-competes rarely hold. I have an abundance mindset and know we can replace the patients if we do our job and I'm happy as long as they are contributing to making the world a better place. I recommend a non-disclosure and these do hold up much better by protecting your proprietary information and your patients' information. Most patients build a relationship with their coach and you stand to lose patients even if they did it the right way.

2) If a team member is not successful in first three months at following the plan no matter how much you/we like them, they are not the right fit to grow the program. Networking and sales are essential skills of the Implementer. Our program is a license program and I don't have the final say but I let each group know very quickly. They may be a good fit as a medical fitness specialist, but the Implementer needs a comprehensive skill set or is showing growth and required areas.

3) Hiring team members without the capacity or skill to run the program because they are a relative, friend or just because the group has seen them as a patient, or because they are more affordable is not a good idea unless they have proven success. For each of our affiliates I will interview all initial candidates as a bonus if they take the fast action scholarship program or start paying for

coaching right away. When I interview, I must determine that they have proven experience or abilities that can be developed as the following four skills are crucial to your Implementers skill set. For one group, I interviewed over 20 candidates before I found someone with these necessary abilities.

    a. They must have proven sales and networking success.

    b. Experience training, retaining and providing results for patients.

    c. Ability to stay organized and process basic administrative functions until able to delegate.

    d. Manage, lead and develop future talent.

4) Owners or Directors that micromanage too much, in areas that do not require micromanaging.

5) Lack of fluid communication between clinic ad gym staff or collaboration. Several Implementers have stated a lack of team work in growing the program and constant pressure with minimal support.

3) What is the biggest marketing mistake you have seen?

Not having a marketing budget of at least $750-$1,000 a month to consistently have print materials, social media and a networking budget. Not maximizing the grass roots strategies to grow outside referrals that are necessary with the launch of the program is a major oversight. In addition, not increasing budget when a positive return is found on any marketing platform. Owners at times can view an increased budget as an expense rather than the immediate and long term growth of the positive return.

4) How much time does the physician or owner need to be involved?

In the beginning, we would like participation with creating the personal marketing story board materials and infographics on the practices proven process. A vision e-mail, why communication statement once made will be part of your long-term marketing strategy. Autoresponders will be used and placed on the website that separates you from other fitness facilities and shows medical oversite. We also need the physician involvement of passing out medical fitness test drive cards to patients during appointments. Groups that have weekly 30 minute meetings regarding key performance indicators and on the monthly call with me have shown grander success. When the Implementer sets up medical referral education meetings in the community this is a significant opportunity for clinic and medical fitness growth when the physician is involved in these education opportunities.

5) Am I able to bring many of my staff members to work with you?

The greater buy-in and development of the entire organization is the more influential impact. We have detailed and advanced training for each provider, billing, IT, administrative, nursing, marketing or business development staff. We want our partners to mimic our path to success while avoiding several of the mistakes we have made along the way.

6) Can you help me hire the right person?

We teach and have a turnkey recruiting system for each partner equipped with job descriptions, compensation plan options, posting templates, prescreen and interview questions, sample offer letters, suggested benefit offerings, compliance modules and where to post.

We recently implemented a fast action scholarship for our programs who start after a discovery and strategy call where we do all the recruiting and interviewing ensuring we have the right candidate with the appropriate skills. This is over a $2,000 value. After this process, we still want each candidate to do an in-person interview to determine harmonization, expectations, personality and core value match. During this key process, we are observing many factors such as being on time and professional during the individual interview and team shadow opportunity before candidate is offered a position.

7) Will you be able to teach me everything your clinic is doing to be successful?

Absolutely! That is the main goal. To increase patient outcomes, profitability and have massive community impact. We implore you to replicate what our team has successfully created. Now nearing eight completed years in practice our model can't be replicated overnight. We created the MedFit's "Medically Fit Practice Success Platform" that is designed to create a highly profitable, scalable, automated and impactful practice in 3 years' time. This includes the Medical Fitness Impact Plan as one of the 5 Pillars. Below is the curriculum for our three-year program. For some groups depending where they are at will be able to complete the curriculum faster and some groups may require more time but the step by step proven process will succeed if executed.

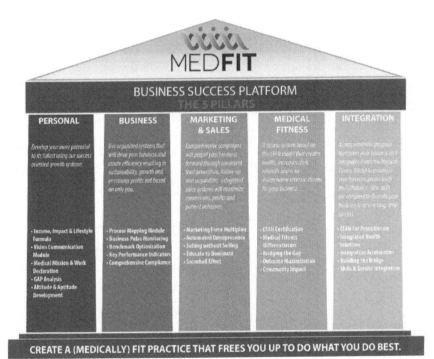

8) What will our group have to create in addition to what comes with your program?

Your original story, mission, core values and scorecard modeling the templates that we have will be requirements to create to measure and ensure success. Creating custom videos and content will also speed the reach of your message and create the community to know, like and trust. Each pillar comes with worksheets, video or audio training, and templates to input your unique information.

To make the full program integrate with your model of healthcare and current systems we will work closely with your group to customize a workflow that will assist in meeting practice goals, objectives and key performance indicators.

9) How do you track success?

One of the first coaching sessions we go through is to establish projections, key performance indicators, tracking mechanisms, and overall scorecards for each team member and department.

You can't manage or improve what you can't measure. You get what you inspect, not what you expect.

10) When do you think all insurances will cover medical fitness?

I believe the writing is on the wall with CMS primed to cover preventative and wellness services starting in 2018 for those meeting specific medical criteria. I believe if solid reporting and tracking metrics are established and with a two-year reporting window this program will prove healthcare savings, medication reduction and greater disease management. I predict all insurances will cover medically supervised training and wellness services for those in the at-risk categories in the coming years.

11) If you could do it all over again what would you do differently?

I would have set up EFT programs from the beginning and never sold bulk sessions. I would have had better incentive based compensation plans for those able to learn how to play a big role in growing our programs. I lost a few good people due to this. I would have also only had 45-minute group training and boot camp programs and 30-minute one-to-one sessions from the start. Very hard to change comp plans or payment plans after the fact without negative ramifications.

12) What are the biggest mistakes you have made?

Not investing in more high level coaching and turn-key programs from the start for other department leaders. This would have saved us from several costly mistakes while instead developing critical skills of the leaders of our company. Each investment besides one has paid 10x the cost of the program. Investing in high level coaching is crucial.

The largest error we made was having our patients submit letters to insurance providers on the benefits we have provided them with our cashed based services in medical fitness, functional medicine and regenerative injections. In 2013 we lost half our insurance contracts due to this. This nearly cost us everything. We have been back in network with all but two payors. Unfortunately, we have helped less people due to this mistake and took a major hit to growth projections we were on pace for. Now we clearly have a "this is not covered" conversation with patients and we prefer shifting our practice to a larger share of cash pay. Cash Services reduce the cost of business and we believe it to be the better medicine in many instances. We like keeping insurance because many office visits, labs and traditional care that we offer is covered. In the future, many of the current cash services we offer will be covered as the evidence is too strong and consumers are demanding these healthcare options. We are not sure we desire that at this time as the reimbursement for PRP or stem cells may be drastically reduced when payors start covering. This will reduce quality when physicians without the proper training start performing these procedures. The pioneers have had years of training bringing this medicine to the point it's at today.

Chapter 9

<u>The 10 Frequently Asked Questions</u>

1) What is the cost to effectively start a medical fitness program? Multiple options are available when it comes to getting started. I would base this decision on four factors.

- Space:
1) Does your existing medical practice have a small room with enough space to start in? If this is the case, then the startup capital needed will be much smaller than investing in a standalone location.

2) If there is no room in your current facility, there is always the option to rent or lease from an existing facility such as a gym, gymnastics facility, or a dance studio. This will carry a very low cost of starting.

3) A standalone facility will require the greatest investment, but will allow the most growth potential other than owning or leasing a space big enough to handle a fully operational fitness and medical facility.

I started training patients in a small room until I was at capacity. At that time, we had two newly hired trainers work out of a Snap Fitness, which was perfect. We paid a monthly membership for each client and Snap appreciated the business. Nine months after starting the medical fitness program we leased our 6,400-square foot standalone building and began leasehold improvements. Three years later we came back together in one large cutting edge health center.

If you are seeking the lowest startup costs, the ideal place to start your program would be in your own facility. It could be in a small room with hardly any startup fee; this is where the Implementer builds up a patient base before another MFS is needed. It's ideal if you have enough space in your existing facility to have everything under one roof. This makes sales, startup, and the cross-referral process much more simplistic. It's also easier for the patient and it makes it possible to bill for more services while a physician is present. Unfortunately, our medical clinic's ability to build out was not an option, so we had to lease a stand-alone facility as we grew.

When the ability to have all services under one roof is not a possibility you could enter an agreement with a small local gym or a box gym as independent contractors within the facility. You would either pay a monthly rent or you would pay a membership fee per client. We have created win-win agreements that help secure gyms to allow our medical practices to start these relationships.

Once you have reached a certain level of patients and your rent from the current facilities is looking close to what you would be paying for a standalone facility, it's time to start researching and locating potentials sites for your new location if you have major growth plans. The previous model can keep you at very low risk and maintaining profitability so we must be certain before we take the next step.

When seeking a standalone facility, it's important that you build a relationship with your realtor. Explain that you are a new facility in need of starting out on the most modest budget possible. This way they are looking for the most affordable starting point that there is. Your location does not have to be commercial unless you have the budget for it. It could be industrial because you are looking for the least minimal startup fee possible. When meeting the owners of the property it's important to let the owner know that your facility will help change the lives of many people, bring more traffic to the area, increase value and the vitality of becoming a local hotspot, bring the area more interest/referrals, and increase the facility's retention rate. Ask the owner what they feel would be fair for the startup cost. There are many other options to help with the startup costs so being resourceful will be advantageous. Many owners will pay the first and last month's rent, pay the build out cost; anything to fill up some of their empty spaces in today's economy. You can also negotiate a lower start rate that increases as your profits increase and cap off at a certain percentage.

- Equipment costs:

In the small room where we started, we had a cable cross machine, Bosu ball, yoga mat, set of interchangeable free weights, three resistance bands, and one treadmill. In location number two we did not incur costs, as we could use the equipment at the Snap Fitness where we provided personal training. We have started programs with as little as $1,000 of equipment up to what we invested. This is not the ultimate factor for success because you can do functional training with minimal equipment. As revenues come in each group can add more equipment to enhance the program platform.

When we created our standalone location, we researched Used Gym Equipment; this is where we purchased all of our equipment at 60% off retail value. We chose the colors we wanted and the equipment we wanted. We paid $64,000 in equipment for well over $160,000 worth of assets. I highly recommend that as soon as you choose a location, you place your order promptly as our experience was the equipment took 3 months to arrive from date of order.

- Fixed expenses:

Fixed expenses are costs of doing business such as your rent, salaried wages, insurance, utilities, employee benefits, office expenses, advertising, telephone, internet, computers, QuickBooks, accounting, bad debt, bank charges, dues and subscriptions, conventions, workman's compensation, legal dues, repair, maintenance, and any lease on equipment.

Many entrepreneurs overlook the "costs of doing business" and do not budget appropriately and is a leading reason many small practices and businesses fail.

- Cost of goods sold:

This is your MFSs' wages. You will only compensate them as they are seeing each patient until your operations get to the size of having full time positions. Cost of goods sold also includes your physical goods sold, such as supplements or pro shop items, payroll tax, and inventory. Cost of goods sold are not a direct expense and they always increase as you grow. You'll find that your payroll and cost of goods sold is always chasing your revenue. Typically, I like a higher COGS if set up properly, and I look to find methods to reduce fixed expenses.

After reviewing the four factors you can easily predict how much startup capital you will need. If you choose to build right away, join The Small Business Association to help secure capital for your facility if you don't have the credit to secure a loan. If you are already established, it should be easy to get a business loan from your local bank. If building, there are several loans and tax incremental financing options you will want to explore to save the most money. If you have the reserve capital it could be started with minimal start-up costs but your monthly operation budget will be anywhere from 4-8k a month if properly investing in the launch of the program.

If you are starting with one of the first two options, you will not need much capital to begin. A loan or available cash flow between $25,000-$50,000 will get you the necessary equipment, should cover all of your fixed expenses, and your cost of goods sold. If you have the right Implementer and infrastructure as explained in this book you will start seeing a return on your investment.

For those of you who plan on starting with the standalone facility, I would recommend about $30,000 for every one thousand square feet of studio space. We required about $180,000 to build out and fund a 6,400-square foot facility when all costs were factored in.

We had $15,000-$20,000 set aside for our first three months of marketing and overhead. We also set aside three months of fixed expenses in case of slow growth for any unforeseen occurrences.

Due to amount of startup costs in the first year, we averaged an $8,500 a month loss at the standalone. This did not include the average of around $67,000 a month of new revenue the medical practice was earning with new and repeat patient services generated from the fitness center.

Very few business models can show a profit in the first year; this model is truly going to revolutionize the medical field in the next 10 years. The Affordable Health Care Act will be eyeing to cut costs and implement new strategies to help patients improve the quality of their life. Medical fitness will be the preventative model that will play an important role in the future of healthcare. This model will help change thousands of lives. It gives our team the opportunity to make a difference, and that is the fulfillment we seek together at Rejuv & MedFit.

2) What are the Stark and anti-kickback considerations with this program?

I will assume that most people reading this book belong to a clinic or a hospital setting that may have many of the legal protections already in place. I will touch on some of the basics, but most of this will pertain to the medical fitness side of a practice. Each state is different and it is highly recommended you seek legal counsel for the proper state and federal regulation that may be applicable to you. The medical fitness model can work for several types of medical practices, although you may have different legal rules and regulations to abide by. Our set-up works as a specialty clinic in sports and orthopedics and is operating with a medical fitness component.

If you are starting your entire practice from the ground floor, your business must be incorporated as a separate entity that you have or would be starting. An example would be "doing business as Joel Baumgartner." This is an absolute must to protect you and your family's assets from any potential legal or financial dispute. It is recommended that you meet with a lawyer and accountant to see which set-up is best for your company. There are different types of set-ups for corporations depending on your business plan.

In many instances, if a partnership is in place there needs to be an exit strategy, and an option to buy out must be a legal agreement stating all parties, responsibilities, stake, and share. This can be accomplished with your attorney

LegalZoom.com can be effective for many of the basic features to get started. I strongly recommend securing a lawyer however to draft all legal documents.

Earlier, I stated the importance of understanding the STARK and anti-kickback regulations in your state. This is a necessary component with this type of model. We have assisted many to navigate thru the very specific questions that need to be asked to your states guidelines to help determine ancillary revenue sharing and referral processes.

Typically, your team of employees will fall under your medical malpractice insurance. It is recommended that you encourage all of your service providers to seek additional liability insurance to protect their own personal interests. There are several agencies that can help you find the best fit for the size and scope of your practice.

An affordable way to set up the proper human resource services is to start with a company like berganKDV, Paychex or ADP or several others to ensure you adhere to the rules and regulations of your state. How you categorize your employees is very important. This is something we provide as consultants, but the content is too broad to go into detail in this book. When your growth allows you to hire an in-house HR team member, all of your structures would already be in place.

3) How soon will it take me to make money?

Depending on your start-up cost selection I have had a few groups be profitable in month one if they were in-house or using another gym. We have customized projection forms we will take you through step by step based on the starting costs and growth model we choose to determine break-even points. I like to put my break-even projections as the one year bench mark however suggest creating capital of a two-year breakeven to prepare for the worst-case scenario. Some new to businesses are under the impression that by just opening a business they will be profitable and making a decent living in no time. Yes, that is possible, typically however not always reality. Frequently, the owner will need to be paid last to properly invest in the resources required to grow a thriving business. I also ask potential investors to try to live a minimalist life while in the early years of business. Ask yourself: What is the essential income or money you need set aside to live off for a period of

12

months and possibly beyond? If the means are not available to do this one may need to consider attaining capital for starting their practice. Instead of pulling money away from the business we want to add to marketing, equipment, staff, and create an infrastructure that will allow you to continue to grow and create a profitable business. I strongly believe that investing in yourself and your practice is better than putting money into savings or other investments that you don't have full control over. Even though I have contributed to investment vehicles, I would rather invest more into myself and company than the stock in some company I do not personally belong to. I strongly state the importance of becoming confident in your ability and what you can produce. When you adopt this mindset, it can take you to the next level in a hurry.

4) Can my PT director or Administrator run the program?

Yes. Anyone can oversee the program and I recommend you have multiple team members who understand the program. However, the success of the program is hinged on the person who is going to sell prospects into programs, network in the community and execute the marketing plan. The person running the program must have more than patient care skills and have the true ability to produce results, but think and operate like a successful business owner. The ability to sell and develop other leaders is a driving force for building a sustainable and successful practice.

5) Is this covered by insurance companies?

The answer is both Yes and No. When patients use clinical services, office visits and labs are typically covered. If injured, Physical Therapy, office visits and procedures are covered if the practice carries insurance. If a patient has any diagnosis such as obesity, diabetes, metabolic syndrome and many more the providers will create a letter of medical necessity so patients can use their health savings accounts or flex dollars. The personal training services would be covered in this instance however most training and health coaching is usually all cash pay. As mentioned earlier CMS will use the DPP to pay for training and wellness services for patients meeting specific criteria.

6) Will the use of these systems help my entire practice?

Yes, without a doubt. In fact, when we first perform a discovery session with potential prospects we need to do the practice assessment mentioned in this book to understand where they are at with their current operations. We created The Medically Fit Practice Success Platform that has 5 Pillars for success. We often have people who join our program go through the first three pillars before we encourage them to start the Medical Fitness Impact Plan. All the pre-work curriculum will lead to practice that is built with a proper foundation.

Experience a Discovery Assessment by going to this website Take your Medically Fit Practice Success Assessment Here: http://www.smartbizquiztribe.com/quiz/1348 to request a Discovery Call and a Practice Assessment Application will be sent to you. Post-completion, we will go over in detail the first three pillars to determine current viability for adding the Medical Fitness Impact Plan to your practice.

7) Can I talk to others who have successfully implemented this program?

Yes, we have past graduates and current affiliates who are enthusiastic to share the success, challenges and benefits of adding medical fitness to you community. Contact me and I will put you in touch with someone of your similar specialty.

8) Can this work for my practice model?

We believe it can work for most medical models. Exercise, nutrition, and mindset are keys to overall health. I don't want to say that it will be successful for all as there are many factors involved and I prefer to do a thorough assessment with each practice who is considering such a model as they may not be seeing the whole picture.

9) Can this be effective and worthy to put in all our other clinics?

Yes. We offer a reduced license fee for each additional location. If the director is overseeing additional locations, there will be no extra coaching fees associated with future locations. I have one franchise group that just implemented the Medical Fitness Impact Plan in their first locations with plans to extend to each location. I have another group that owns over twenty clinics that we are in the beginning phases of breaking ground with their strategy of growth.

10) What are your costs if I request your services?

Great question. This is not an easy answer on paper and that is why a Discovery Call is preferred to give you the best idea on what option is best for you at the current moment. Nearly half of our affiliates we started the process of "The Medically Fit Practice Success Platform" to work on the first 3 Pillars of the foundation for success before integrating medical fitness. Our fee is $1,000 per month for all of our coaching programs. This is an online curriculum that you can systematically and quickly adjust our forms, templates and materials and rebrand then implement into your clinic.

Once we have made headway and most of your foundation is in place we start the Medical Fitness Impact Plan. The license is $12K for the "done for you" program and web build out. If you spent 3 months previously coaching, we reduce your license fee by the 3K as that was your original interest in joining us but we must make sure your practice is prepared for growth and scaling. After this timeframe, you would continue the coaching fee as well at the $1K a month investment. Once you have been with us for 12 months the coaching fee drops to $500 a month and you will stay locked in at that rate if you desire. Because this is a license program and not a franchise you can discontinue the coaching anytime you feel you can operate successfully on your own. I have had two groups just buy the license as they felt they had the team to operate the program successfully on their own. I think it's a mistake to drop after two years as my team and I continue to attend masterminds to stay current with the best marketing and automation secrets in the industry. This year alone I'm in involved in three different masterminds with different focuses to grow our organization and my skills. Everything we learn we bring forward to our affiliates to help create health worldwide as we are committed to knowledge-sharing.

When we get to 50 locations we are going to increase our one-time license fee to 20K as we have invested thousands of hours and hundreds of thousands of dollars compiling this life changing program. We have priced ourselves within your means. We have focused on mastering our delivery and system to better provide success for all our affiliates. From the bottom of our hearts we thank each pioneer who has taken a leap with us, all in the efforts to fix a broken healthcare system and create health in our communities and throughout the world.

We offer four incentives to affiliates seeking to reduce overall investment:

1)Fast Action Scholarship: We believe in fast and imperfect action is a key to success. I'm not talking about being sloppy and not doing your due diligence on any investment but trusting your gut, taking daily action towards your goals and dreams and always course correcting as soon as we get a little off track. This is a little uncomfortable for some physicians however you don't have other physicians critiquing your programs. Consumers don't want prefect or pedestal perfect pictures. They want content, relatability, emotional connection and you. Those that start after the strategy call, which is the call after the Discovery Call awards prospects a 3K fast action scholarship. Even if you're not ready for the Medical Fitness Impact Plan and need a few months of pre-work we will discount your license fee when you are ready to fully begin. Each of our programs come with a full money back guarantee if after 3 months you do not feel 100% comfortable that we are going to make your practice successful or for whatever reason we do not over deliver on what we have promised. We have never had this happen although we put it out there that we are not shortsighted or ever comfortable with not operating within our core values.

2) Paid in Full: Anyone who pays in full will receive $2K off the full price.

3) Out of Country Discount: It is our goal to spread the Medical Fitness Impact Plan worldwide so the first affiliate in any new country other than the U.S.A. will receive a $2K discount.

4) Referral Program: Once we have proven our value to you and you recommend us to any clinics that join our mission we will provide you with a 1K referral bonus. That escalates by $500 for each additional affiliate that joins.

Each of the discounts and incentives can be combined to minimize investment.

We are commencing a franchise of MedFit in 2018. We are diligently beginning the process now. The difference in this model is our partners must take our name and we will execute the marketing, billing and management process versus just giving all of our materials, course work and coaching for the practices. This will come at a higher expense including the yearly franchise fee and royalty fee however we will be providing much more hands on service. We plan to continue to offer our license model with all of the same value nevertheless the franchise will have a much greater brand recognition, marketing and management value.

MedFit Options	WEEKEND TRAINING $2,500	MASTERMIND $10,000 PIF OR $1,000 / MO	LICENSE $10,000 LIC $1,000 / $500 MO
BRANDED WEBSITE / UNIVERSITY	X	X	✔
MEDICAL FITNESS SYSTEM	X	X	✔
COACHING CALLS / MONTH	X	1	2
VISIT TO HDQTRS / TRAINING	X	2 DAYS SHADOW	3 DAYS TRAINING
MASTERMINDS	1	3	X
YEARLY REGENERATIVE SUMMIT	X	✔	✔
WEEKLY GROUP WEBINARS	X	✔	✔
REJUV BUSINESS SYSTEM	X	✔	✔
REGEN. INJECTION TRAINING	✔	✔	X
VENDOR / GROUP DISCOUNTS	✔	✔	✔
MASTERMIND (GSD AWARD ELIG.)	X	✔	X

Chapter 10

The 5 Myths of Medical Fitness

1) This will take too much time for the physicians or owners. The physicians or providers see the patients that the program generates but have very little to do with the operations or success of the program. The Implementer and fitness team will do nearly all the execution. However, if the owner/physician will create videos or e-mails that they model from the templates we have created, success will be much more elevated for the community to understand your brand. I have worked with one practice that did not want new patients as was completely full and the reason she started the program was as a concierge service to give her patients better outcomes and provide her additional ancillary income. She realized she was not capturing a revenue source that she was actively telling each one of her patients to do...exercise and start eating healthy, focus on nutrition.

The one thing we encourage our providers to do in the room that takes least then one minute is to ask two questions as a vital sign in the EHR:

1) "On Average, How Many Days Per Week Do You Engage in Moderate to Strenuous Exercise (Like a Brisk Walk)?"

2) "On Average, How Many Minutes Do You Engage in Exercise at This Level?"

GOAL: 150 Minutes/ Week of Moderate to Intense Activity

After that we provide a physical hand-out to Rejuv University and offer a free Medical Fitness Test Drive.

2) Patients won't be compliant so why encourage them to eat healthy and exercise?

In medical journals and reviews I have read I see this garbage message all the time. To me it's an excuse to ignore our obligation as medical providers to enlighten patients of their health risks. Studies show the opposite of what I have heard.

Patients Who Were Counseled by Their Physician, were more Motivated to Attempt Weight Loss and Had a Better Understanding of Their Health Risk. (Acad Med. 2004; 79:156-161)

Were 3 Times more Likely to Attempt Weight Loss than Those Who Reported Not Receiving Advice. (JAMA. 1999; 282:1576-1578)

3) That there is little money to be made with medical fitness. We can show that nearly 75% of all of our income stems from medical fitness. Each of my speaking opportunities and travels I have yet to see a solo owner independent practice with as much success, growth and impact as ours in such short timeframe. Waite Park, Minnesota and the surrounding area where we are from is not very large. The median income is $47K and a very conservative market. I will agree the fitness side on its own is not going to make you rich. It can provide impressive cash flow and net income if you acquire the right person and follow our guidelines. The greatest benefit this will provide is growing your practice with motivated patients who are actively working to get better.

4) People can't afford cash-based services and my market is not right for this.

Show me any area where people are not going to gyms, hiring personal trainers, or spending their money on things that do not provide health and happiness. You can put myself or any of the better fitness professionals that I have worked with anywhere in the world and we could grow a successful program. It will be the capability of the person selling the program to provide the hope and the possible transformation with your patients. I hear the same thing about regenerative medicine and functional medicine doctors giving excuses that people can't afford their services. You/we must look in the mirror. I'm not talking hard sales; I'm referring to giving people what they want and generating results. You want me to prove you wrong? Hire me to come to your clinic and put patients in front of me for any of your services and I will help them get started if I understand your program and it improves people. I could never sell something I don't fully believe in my heart can help someone as that would go against my core values and when you operate outside that realm it is not good for the soul.

5) This is very easy to make work.

I have provided each one of the primary contributing factors in this book to guide you to success. I can't call it easy because we have been diligently committed, however it has been easy to work hard because of the passion we all have for the service we are providing.
You will need to grow; your staff will need to grow and get a little uncomfortable along the way.

In closing, each time I visit with fitness or medical practice owners I enjoy the opportunity to end each talk with my tips for success. It's a ten-minute talk. E-mail frontdesk@rejuvmedical.com and we will send you the audio file to this closing that describes each of the tips for success.

1) 3 P'S: Passion, Purpose and Persistence Must Be Your Driving Force

2) Work Harder and More Focused than Others Are Willing

3) Take Self Responsibility for Everything in Your Life

4) Don't Reinvent: Model and Build Your Differentiating Factors

5) Learn Systems if You Plan to Scale

6) Marketing and Sales Helps Your Family, Community, Nation and World

7) Continue to Educate and Grow Outside Your Comfort Zone

8) Change the Way You Think When Your Mind Doesn't Serve You

9) Become a Giver, Leader and Developer of Other Leaders

10) Decrease Stress in Your Life and Business

11) Surround Yourself with Success

12) Become an Effective Communicator

Chapter 11

The Benefits of The Medical Fitness I.M.P.A.C.T. Plan

1) Create real health for patients by aiding to reverse chronic disease and improve outcomes in clinical settings.

2) Make an undeniable difference in your community and, thus, be the "go-to" within your niche.

3) Lead the mission to change the direction of our health care crisis by being proactive by adding conservative, integrative and preventative medicine through nutrition and fitness services.

4) Mission and purpose drive a TEAM that is on fire to make a difference.

5) It is easy to add to any current clinic size if there is existing office or PT space.

6) Low overhead options and no risk propositions.

7) You don't have to build It. The Implementer leads the implementation.

8) Build a practice that isn't fully dependent on provider income!

9) DECREASE the NEED for MEDICATIONS that DON'T address the root of several medical issues, NO BANDAIDS.

10) Diversify and build a practice that is cash model friendly.

11) Outcome and bundled payment models are the future.

12) Create constant new referrals to their existing practice.

13) Incredible marketing and patient attractor for your practice.

14) Highly motivated population make enhanced patients and outcomes.

15) Extreme cross referral synergy that benefits all departments.

16) Medical fitness patients become lifelong patients. Because you change their lives, your patients will become your best raving fans.

17) Medical clinics can use position of authority to attract patients into a practice using medical oversight USP (unique selling position).

18) Compliment a current medical practice to increase revenue and obtain new patients. Medically supervised weight loss captures an untouched market.

19) Stay a step ahead of the competition by being the first in your area in the medical fitness market. Differentiation is essential in a competitive niche.

20) For the first-time CMS, will utilize the "Diabetes Prevention Program." This insurance program will cover wellness services for patients with pre-diabetes, diabetes and metabolic syndrome.

Chapter 12

Why Is Now the Time to Add Medical Fitness?

1) The health crisis and obesity epidemic is here to stay until preventative measures are put in place and better utilized.

2) The rising costs to practices will only continue. Practices will continue to be pressured to meet with more patients and passive income streams will need to be maximized.

3) Consumers are seeking better care and looking for solutions that improve outcomes and not just another cover up.

4) The opportunity is now to create change in a several hundred-billion-dollar weight loss industry. Physicians have an unrivaled (USP) unique selling position leveraging their expertise and authority with patients.

5) Those that win in the stock market can see emerging trends and gaps and there is a significant shortage and demand for preventative services.

The mission of the robust and transparent overview is to provide the vision of key elements as you add medical fitness to your practice. Please click below to take the Medically Fit Practice Success Assessment and apply to see if you qualify for a no-cost Discovery and Strategy session.

Take your Medically Fit Practice Success Assessment Here: http://www.smartbizquiztribe.com/quiz/1348

In Friendship,

J.R. Burgess

Made in the USA
San Bernardino, CA
28 December 2017